100 Years that Shaped the Countryside:

A century of campaigns by
CPRE Peak District and South Yorkshire

Edited and written by Bill Bevan

Based on the Account of Sixty-Six Years' Work 1924 to 1989,
annual reports 1990 – 2022, CPRE newsletters' and the Peakland Guardian.

With contributions by Judith Calvert, Charles MacDonald-Jones,
Marianne Morgan and Andy Tickle.

Published by CPRE Peak District and South Yorkshire to celebrate its centenary in 2024.

Contents

3	Foreword
5	Acknowledgements
6	A Century for the Countryside
9	First Steps - 1924-1933
15	The Good, the Bad and the Ugly
20	The Beautiful Frame and Beyond - 1934-1943
26	The Fight for Sheffield's Green Belt
31	The Birth of National Parks - 1944-1953
36	Growth Gathers No Moss - 1954-1963
43	Shaping Post-War Planning Policy
47	Progress Under Assault - 1964-1973
54	A National Park Motorway - 1974-1983
62	Long and Winding Roads
68	From Commercial Development to Renewable Energy - 1984-1993
74	New Challenges - 1994-2003
80	Digging in Against Quarries
87	Quarrying out the National Park - 2004-2013
93	Energy - A Tale of Two Centuries
99	Hard Campaigns and Happy Celebrations - 2014-2024
107	The Future
108	Presidents, Chairs, Honorary Secretaries and Honorary Treasurers.

Foreword

We are a charity that has campaigned to promote, enhance and protect the landscapes and green spaces of the Peak District and South Yorkshire for a century. We believe a beautiful, sustainable countryside is important for everyone. We work to:

- **connect people and countryside;** so that more people can enjoy the benefits of the countryside.

- **promote rural life;** so that the countryside and its communities thrive.

- **empower communities;** so that people can help improve and protect their local environment.

- **grow our capacity;** so that our work can continue now and in the future for generations to come.

Underpinning this is our commitment to tackle the climate and nature emergencies, which sits at the heart of everything we do.

This account of the key campaigning achievements of our charity follows in the tradition of those we produced each decade up until the end of the 1980s *(the collated 1924 - 1989 account is viewable on our website)*. It is by no means a detailed account of everything we do, rather it illustrates the breadth and depth of our work since our foundation on 7 May 1924 when a *'small and select gathering of like-minded men and women, disturbed by the increasing defacement of the beauty of the Peak District by 'incongruous and promiscuous development', met at Endcliffe Vale House in the quiet western suburbs of Sheffield'.*

No account of our charity can be made without recording the debt we owe to the vision and drive of Ethel Haythornthwaite. As Ethel Gallimore she founded the charity, with the encouragement and financial support of her parents and siblings, and with her husband Gerald Haythornthwaite played an immense role in advocating for and protecting the landscapes of the Peak District and around Sheffield. Moreover, every one of the campaigns in this book was the work of many staff, volunteers, advisors and supporters, and we are indebted to each and every one of them for everything they have done in support of our work over the last one hundred years.

It is our task to ensure that the charity created and supported by their efforts, devotion and generosity continues to campaign with the same vision, effectiveness and professionalism to protect the landscapes and green spaces of the Peak District and South Yorkshire for everyone. We take on that task with joy, drawn from the inspiration of our forbears and our passion for a beautiful, sustainable future.

Dame Fiona Reynolds

Acknowledgements

CPRE Peak District and South Yorkshire are grateful to the people who have brought this book together. Bill Bevan for researching publications, annual reports and campaign papers from which to edit and write the text, and select the photographs. Andy Tickle for working with Bill to set the format for the book, provide insight into past campaigns and comment on the text. Tomo Thompson for managing and advising on the content; Susan Belt, Rebecca Simpson and Gemma Thorpe for assistance with the digital archive and images held at the office. Tim Knebel at Sheffield Archives and Melanie Collier at Derbyshire Record Office, for advising on the contents of CPRE and Friends of the Peak District collections.

We are indebted to every one of the many staff, volunteers, advisors and supporters for everything they have done in support of our work to campaign for the countryside over the last one hundred years.

1 | A Century for the Countryside

From top left. The Mayfield Valley today, part of Sheffield's green belt, 1930s.
Ethel Haythornthwaite visiting the Peak District with other members of the national parks Hobhouse Committee, 1940s. Gerald Haythornthwaite's impression of a motorway through Longdendale, 1970s. Fracking site at Woodsetts, Rotherham, 2010s.

One hundred years of countryside campaigns. A constant checking of planning applications and choosing which to respond to. Attending public inquiry after public inquiry to make the case for the countryside. Time and time again, reading through densely written local plans, regional strategies and national planning guidance to influence what is built and where. There has been no rest, no stone left unturned.

When Ethel Haythornthwaite (then Gallimore) founded the Sheffield Association for the Protection of Local Scenery in 1924 there were no planning controls, green belts or national parks. The only Peak District property owned by the National Trust was Winster Market Hall. Since then, CPRE Peak District and South Yorkshire has, under different names and with different people, fought hard to protect some corner of a local field as forever undeveloped. Many corners have been fought, countless campaigns won and lost.

This book is a celebration of those campaigns and a recognition of the hard work of the many people who have worked for CPRE Peak District and South Yorkshire. As we journey through time, we see what issues preyed most on the minds of countryside campaigners, and list the branch's achievements. As we do so, we encounter new challenges to the countryside and see time and again those threats that do not go away.

Our starting point is a small book, published by the branch in 1989 called *Account of Sixty-Six Years' Work 1924 to 1989*. It divided the 66 years into decades, except for one chapter that stretched its remit to 15 years. Each decade opened with a summary of threats and branch work called The Situation, then went on to list key achievements and feature a small selection of major successes in more depth. We have followed this structure, honoured the decisions taken and kept the words written by the book's author who, though not given, we assume was Gerald Haythornthwaite. Gerald was then the branch Honorary Secretary, a leading countryside campaigner since 1936 and husband of Ethel until she died in 1986. We have filled in some gaps and extended the review of campaigns from 1989 to 2024, keeping to the same format and retaining the phrase The Situation to introduce each decade. To do so, we have gone back to branch annual reports, newsletters, Peakland Guardians and archived campaign papers.

We see the new challenges to the countryside that have had to be confronted and solved over the last 100 years. At the end of the First World War and the death of her first husband, Ethel became a keen walker. She noticed new developments spurred on by the increase in motor vehicles, which gave greater access to the countryside and enabled more people to live outside the cities. Petrol stations, advertising hoardings and the groundwork for ribbon developments of new houses were springing up. Litter became an issue. One of her first campaigns was to persuade buses to carry litter bins for tickets. Protecting land through ownership was a key way to prevent development before planning controls. Ethel used an inheritance and was behind fundraising campaigns that bought and gifted large areas of moorland to Sheffield Corporation (the forerunner of the City Council) and the National Trust. The Longshaw Estate is an early and magnificent example. The housing boom that followed the Second World War, out-of-town retail parks, mobile phone masts, windfarms and fracking have all marched over the horizon at different times.

Some issues endure. Inappropriate development in green belts, the quality of building design, quarrying, energy infrastructure and transport have all had to be faced throughout most of the branch's 100 years. A major road through Longdendale is as significant an issue today as it was 50 years ago when a motorway across the national park was first proposed. How we produce and transport energy has been a constant, with intrusive pylons and overhead wires still a live topic.

We also publish several thematic studies of threats and campaigns that have been important throughout the 100 years. These were written by community researchers who volunteered their time on the CPRE Peak District and South Yorkshire Archive project in 2022.

The voice of this book moves between the 1980s and today, from contemporary annual reports to those of us looking back over the history of branch activities. Text is by Bill Bevan, sometimes edited from branch publications, except where other authors are cited or sources of branch publications are named.

One hundred years of campaign successes soar out of these pages like the Peak District's highest hills rise above mist, a testament to the vision and perseverance first shown by Ethel Haythornthwaite, who is recognised by having the loftiest of those hills named after her.

2 | First Steps – 1924-1933

Ethel and Gerald Haythornthwaite.

The Situation

Our Society was formed in 1924 as the Sheffield Association for the Protection of Local Scenery and was supported privately until 1937 when a generous legacy from the late Julius Kayser made our Society self-supporting at that time.

In 1927 the Society accepted the Council for the Preservation of Rural England's invitation to become their representative in the Peak District. During the first decade of our activity, there was no effective planning system. It was not until 1st April 1933 that local authorities were permitted by the Town and County Planning Act 1932 to prepare planning schemes and if they so resolved to regulate development. They could not however prevent development for the sake of amenity without incurring the penalty of compensation.

In our first Report covering the years 1924 to 1931, we noted *"that the chief cause of the present rural disfigurement is uncontrolled building development which is often entirely out of harmony with the character of its natural surroundings."*

Our work was therefore directed to:

- Drawing public attention to the beauty of the Peak District countryside and to the accelerating damage caused by uncontrolled development.
- Persuading local authorities, builders and other developers to design and choose materials for buildings appropriate to their setting in the Peak District.
- Organising the purchase of areas of outstanding natural beauty in the Peak District for safekeeping by the National Trust and to forestall unsuitable building development.

Source: *Account of Sixty-Six Years' Work 1924 to 1989.*

Some of our Achievements and Campaigns

Publications

1930 *Building in the Peak District.*

1932 *The Threat to the Peak* (90 pages and 150 illustrations).

1934 *Housing in the Peak District* (A manual on the design and layout and choice of materials for houses in the Peak District).

Exhibitions

1929 Save the Countryside shown at the Cutlers' Hall, Sheffield.

1933 *Building Materials Suitable for the Peak District* a permanent exhibition.

Land Purchases

1927 The Duke of Rutland's Longshaw Lodge and 744 acres were presented to the National Trust in 1931, the first acquisition of land by the National Trust in the Peak District.

1933 Blacka Moor, 448 acres, purchased by Alderman J. G. Graves, a member of our Society, and presented to the City of Sheffield.

Improvement of Building Design

1930 Joint CPRE/RIBA/IOB Peak District Advisory Panel of Architects established under our auspices.

1933 Qualified architect/planner appointed to our staff.

1935 Portfolio of working drawings compiled from designs selected by competition among local architects for sale to builders.

Source: *Account of Sixty-Six Years' Work 1924 to 1989.*

How We Made a Difference

Founding the Sheffield Association for the Protection of Local Scenery, 1924

The founding of the Association in 1924 was the vision of Ethel Haythornthwaite. The Association brought people together who shared her determination to protect the countryside around Sheffield from harmful development. It brought skills and knowledge to the cause and gave a voice to the countryside which could raise awareness and galvanise others to act.

The Association identified the challenges and threats to the countryside, undertook campaigns, developed solutions and put them into action. Ethel and other members of the Association knew those in power, to talk to, work with and argue against, as well as those with influence and the finances to help with land purchases.

Preservation through Purchase, 1927-1933

Left: Longshaw. Right: Blacka Moor looking towards Sheffield.

The Duke of Rutland's Longshaw Lodge Estate of 11,533 acres was put up for auction in July 1927 without restrictions. This Estate comprised Longshaw Lodge, a ducal shooting lodge with formal gardens and park, woodlands and farms, amounting to 747 acres surrounded by 10,786 acres of high moorlands of great natural beauty and much archaeological interest. The prospectus for the sale advertised the parklands as suitable for a golf course and the woodland as affording several *"beautifully placed building sites".*

The accessibility of the Estate to Sheffield and the enjoyment it might provide for its inhabitants in its scenic, natural history and archaeological riches made its preservation from building development and its public availability imperative.

Fortunately, the adjoining Local Authorities of Sheffield and Chesterfield resolved to acquire the major part of the high moorlands for water gathering grounds; and, upon the initiative of Mr W. Elliott Dixon, Secretary of the Sheffield Council of Social Service, a Joint Committee of his Council and our Society, the Sheffield Association for the Protection of Local Scenery, under the Chairmanship of Mr J. H. Doncaster, resolved to purchase Longshaw Lodge and its grounds of 747 acres.

This was effected through the good offices of Sheffield Corporation making the initial purchase of the lodge and grounds and subsequently conveying them to the Joint Committee Upon the payment of £13,000 raised by a bank overdraft. The sale was completed on 29th September 1927. Five months later £9,208 had been raised by the Joint Committee toward the repayment of the overdraft, subscribed largely by generous gifts from members of our Society and the Sheffield Town Trustees. Two public appeals assisted by the Sheffield Ramblers' Association and a further generous gift from the Sheffield Town Trustees made possible the conveyance of the Estate on 25th March 1931 to the National Trust who paid the outstanding amount on a mortgage of £1,339.

Sheffield Corporation's purchase of the Houndkirk and Burbage Moors was accompanied by a restrictive covenant with the Joint Committee against building development other than that required for their own water-gathering ground purposes. This effectively protected the entire prospect of countryside seen from Longshaw Lodge and its grounds which include the Burbage Valley and the summits of Carts Wark and Higgar Tor.

One part of the Estate, Blacka Moor, of 448 acres close to the outskirts of Sheffield at Dore and Tolley, providing a majestic prospect of moorland hills and woodland on the western approaches to the city, was acquired privately for building development. The new owner's intention was in his own words *"not to allow any building other than Derbyshire Stone and that preference would be given to Sheffield people willing to build artistic cottages not more than four to the acre."* This would nevertheless have extended the suburbs of Sheffield sporadically into the moorland hills of the Peak District to their great detriment. Development of Blacka Moor was delayed by the adoption in 1929 of a draft Town Planning Scheme by Norton Rural District Council designating the area as a private open space which the new owner announced the intention to resist.

There being no certainty that this designation would hold, an approach was made in 1932 by our Honorary Secretary, to the late Alderman J.G. Graves, J.P., the generous benefactor to the City of Sheffield in so many ways and a member of our Society, with a view to his purchasing Blacka Moor and preventing any building development. After a visit to the property guided by our Honorary Secretary, he made an offer for its purchase which was accepted, and in 1933 he presented Blacka Moor to the City of Sheffield as an open space for the enjoyment of its inhabitants in perpetuity.

Source: *Account of Sixty-Six Years' Work 1924 to 1989.*

The Threat to the Peak, 1932

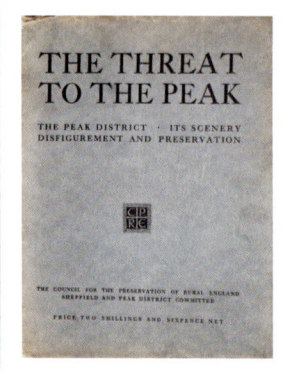

The Threat to the Peak was a major statement about uncontrolled development in the Peak District, over 20 years before the region was to be designated as a national park. It is credited as edited by E.B.G. - Ethel Haythornthwaite under her name of the time - Ethel Bassett Gallimore.

The book is beautifully illustrated with black and white photographs, showing how the branch used the power of imagery to achieve its goals. The first chapter sets the scene, literally, with a description of the scenery of the Peak District. It then explores the main threats to the region in 12 short chapters, each ending with captioned photographs to emphasise the points made. Solutions are put forward for each threat. The twelfth chapter is about the lack of land under the ownership of the National Trust and the purchase of Longshaw to counter a Sheffield city proposal to

build a reservoir in the Burbage Valley. Longshaw was gifted to the National Trust and is an important destination for thousands of Sheffield residents to escape the city and benefit from the open countryside. Like many students, taking the bus to Fox House to walk at Longshaw was the author's first taste of the Peak District after arriving in Sheffield.

The threats identified in the book vary in scale and many will be familiar to us today – buildings, advertising hoardings, litter, wildflower preservation, bird protection, petrol stations, road building, bridges, electricity cables, rubbish tips and industry. Some of these highlight major new developments, such as the increase in private car ownership, that were impacting the Peak District at the time. Petrol stations and roads were built to satisfy the growing demand and while building petrol stations was a particularly historical phenomenon, road building continues to fill the inbox of countryside campaigners today.

The book finishes with a statement of the need for effective town and country planning.

3 | The Good, the Bad and the Ugly
By Judith Calvert

Early CPRE Peak District and South Yorkshire publications about buildings in the Peak District. Copyright Bill Bevan.

What do you consider to be the main threat to the countryside today? Perhaps climate change or inappropriate development, road building or litter? If you had asked the same question a century ago, the answer would have been one word: ugliness.

The Sheffield Association for the Protection of Local Scenery was alarmed by the increasing threat to the beauty of the Peak District on their doorstep. They began raising awareness through lectures and exhibitions, letters and publications. The 'beautiful and the ugly' was a theme that appeared regularly over the coming decades.

The Threat of Ugliness

The timing of their campaign to save the countryside from 'ugliness' was not a coincidence. The 1920s was a period of rapid change. More people owned cars and enjoyed trips to the countryside; some were keen to relocate permanently. There was pressure to widen roads and replace bridges and 'ugly and ill-placed' petroleum filling stations appeared. Advertisement hoardings sprang up, littering increased and refuse tips were a problem. Amenities such as electricity and telephones, requiring pylons and poles, spread to rural areas. Modern industries based in the countryside, such as quarrying, expanded.

But the chief cause of 'rural disfigurement' for the campaigners was uncontrolled building development. This was *"often entirely out of harmony with the character of its natural surroundings"* according to the Association's 1931 Annual Report. With no effective planning legislation, no national park and no green belt, there was little in place to stop ugly and out-of-place buildings.

The Threat to the Peak

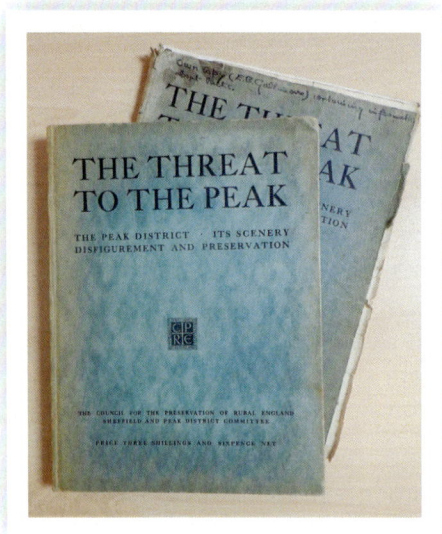

As seen in the previous chapter, *The Threat to the Peak* included short chapters on each of the main threats. The author of the chapter on buildings did not hold back: *"Hundreds of vulgar villas, complete with fussy facades, creep up the hills out of Sheffield, and odd specimens of the same type shatter the harmony of remote villages. Pink bungalows suddenly appear in the heart of a wooded dale or austere moor, ruining acres of noble scenery."*

The author went on to explain the impact that inappropriate building had on the landscape before highlighting the need for public 'enlightenment' and the responsibility of local authorities. Photographs showed traditional buildings alongside 'suitable' and 'unsuitable' modern buildings.

Including 'suitable' modern buildings was important. The Committee was not simply 'anti' everything modern. It accepted that new affordable houses had to be built and that many of these would have to be in rural settings.

Housing in the Peak District

More detailed advice arrived in 1934 with the publication of *Housing in the Peak District* — the forerunner of the modern 'Design Guide'. The authors explained that old buildings in rural areas were constructed of materials found in the neighbourhood — in the Peak District this meant stone — and had a distinct local style. Buildings  were also designed to fit their location — *"they seem to grow naturally out of their surroundings and to increase their beauty."* Modern buildings often ignore these factors in their choice of materials (including colour), design and location.

The main aim of *Housing in the Peak District* was not to criticise, but to suggest designs which would harmonise with the old buildings and the landscape. Local stone was too expensive to be used as a regular building material, so the authors recommended inexpensive alternatives. These were listed in an appendix, complete with suggested suppliers and a price list. Suitable building materials were available for viewing at the Committee's headquarters.

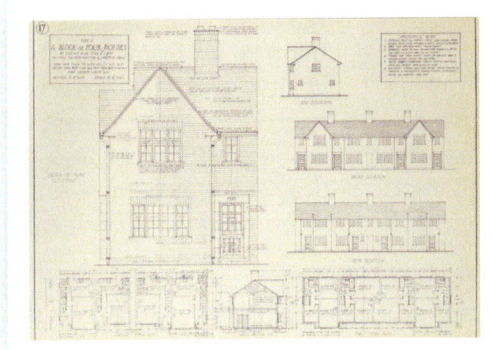

Small Houses and Bungalows for the Peak District

Further practical help from the Committee came with the compilation of a portfolio of drawings of inexpensive houses and bungalows. These were presented in an easily accessible form in *Small Houses and Bungalows suitable for the Peak District* published in 1936. The illustrations consist of an 'artist's impression' of the houses, floor plans, materials, and approximate building costs.

Legal Protection

Alongside this work, the Committee had campaigned hard for the establishment of the Sheffield green belt and the Peak District National Park. The Town and Country Planning Act was passed in 1947. But despite these successes, the pressures on the countryside continued.

The Case for Preservation

The campaigners felt it was necessary to keep making the intellectual case for preserving 'natural beauty'. In 1966, forty years after his wife had founded the Sheffield Association, Gerald Haythornthwaite gave a talk on the BBC Home Service. His subject was 'My Case for Preservation' and he began by stating: *"The most noticeable characteristic of the 19th and 20th centuries, and especially the 20th, is ugliness."*

Gerald was concerned about irreparable damage to the countryside from industrial activity and the loss of regional diversity in the rural landscape. He argued that people needed to connect with nature, not just for 'delight and inspiration' but also for their mental wellbeing – a strikingly modern idea. A BBC producer wrote afterwards that the talk was *"one of the most successful we have broadcast for some time"*.

Letters of appreciation from listeners and other articles by Gerald on the theme of 'rural beauty' and its survival are preserved in the archives of CPRE Peak District and South Yorkshire, now housed in Sheffield Archives.

Beauty Today

Many of the issues familiar to the pioneer campaigners are still with us today. The work of CPRE Peak District and South Yorkshire includes planning and transport issues, quarrying, overhead powerlines and litter and fly-tipping, alongside challenges such as the climate emergency. The branch has many practical ideas for what you can do. It also continues to advocate for high standards in landscape and building design.

And while ugliness is perhaps not a word we use today when speaking about the threat to the countryside, the campaign to preserve natural beauty which Ethel and Gerald Haythornthwaite and their fellow campaigners started is very much ongoing. The aim of CPRE Peak District and South Yorkshire remains to promote the beauty, tranquillity and diversity of the countryside in the Peak District and South Yorkshire for everyone to enjoy now and in the future.

4 | The Beautiful Frame and Beyond - 1934-1943

The Mayfield Valley, part of Sheffield's green belt, then and in 2020.

The Situation

The Local Authorities began to prepare planning schemes and regulations to control the appearance of buildings under the Town and Country Planning Act of 1932. They made use of the services of our Peak District Advisory Panel of Architects, through our Society's architect, for advice on the control of designs and choice of materials for new buildings. They were however still unable to preserve land permanently from building development for the sake of amenity without liability to pay compensation.

Our main occupations were:

- The promotion of a green belt for Sheffield.
- The designation of a national park for the Peak District.
- The protection of these areas from unsuitable development.

Source: *Account of Sixty-Six Years' Work 1924 to 1989.*

Some of our Achievements and Campaigns

Publications

1936 *Small Houses and Bungalows*, illustrating by plans and perspective drawings the portfolio of designs available for sale.

Exhibitions

1937 Second *Save the Countryside* exhibition shown at the Graves Art Gallery, Sheffield, (16,000 visitors) and subsequently at Buxton Pavilion Gardens, Stafford, Mansfield, Derby, Burton and Hanley Art Galleries, Norton and Bakewell Agricultural Shows and in Rotherham and Chesterfield.

Promotion of a Green Belt for Sheffield

1935 Deputation to Sheffield City Council to secure a green belt for the City.

1937 Sheffield Green Belt surveyed and mapped by our officers.

1938 Resolution by Sheffield Corporation adopting a provisional green belt substantially in accordance with our recommendations.

Damaging residential development successfully resisted

1935 93 acres between Whirlow Bridge and Dore Moor Inn.

1936 14 acres of the grounds of Whiteley Wood Hall.

Promotion of the Peak District as a National Park

1938 The Voluntary Joint Committee for the Peak National Park was established under our auspices to promote a national park for the Peak District.

1939 Boundaries for a Peak District National Park surveyed and mapped.

Damaging development successfully resisted

1939 The Winnats Pass, construction of a graded motor road by Derbyshire County Council.

1939   Edale, the Old Mill, erection of a steelworks on a 50 acre site.

Land purchased and presented or covenanted to the National Trust

1934/36   Longshaw Estate, a further 268 acres including Surprise View.

1937   Harpur Lees Farm, Derwent Valley, 34 acres.

1937   Coppice Wood, Derwent Valley, 11 acres.

1938   Froggatt Wood, adjacent to Longshaw, 76 acres.

1941   Lees and Orchard Farms, Edale Valley, 300 acres.

1942   Edale End Farm, Edale Valley, 91 acres.

1942   Mam Tor and the Winnats Pass, 473 acres.

Source: *Account of Sixty-Six Years' Work 1924 to 1989.*

How We Made a Difference
Sheffield Green Belt, 1935-38

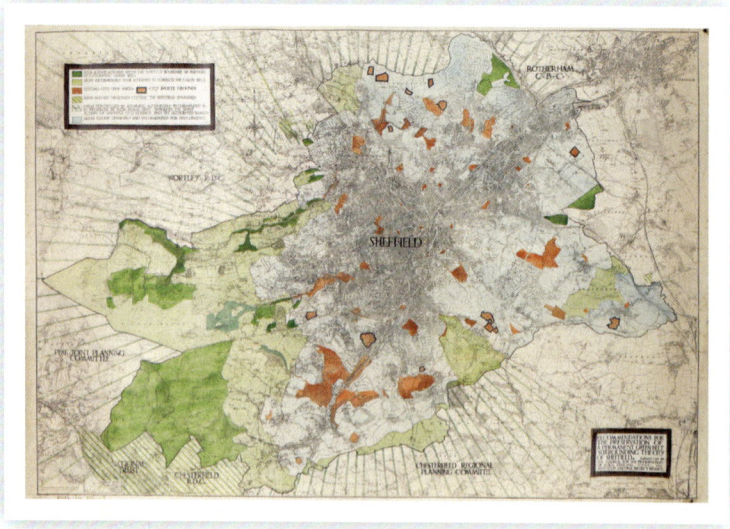

The Sheffield Green Belt has been one of the branch's major achievements of the last 100 years. CPRE Peak District and South Yorkshire was instrumental in pushing this forward during the 1930s. The branch lobbied Sheffield Corporation directly and surveyed the land around Sheffield. This showed the undeveloped land around the city, which the branch used to submit a plan for the Green Belt which would encircle the city and maintain farmland, woodland and moorland within easy distance of Sheffield residents. The campaign resulted in Sheffield Corporation accepting the proposal in 1938.

Early preservation of the Green Belt was secured through land purchases by Sheffield Corporation and J.G. Graves, who gifted his properties to the city. Much of the Mayfield Valley was secured in this way.

Since then, CPRE Peak District and South Yorkshire has been at the forefront of fighting proposals to develop on Sheffield's Green Belt, sometimes with success and sometimes not. The city's ownership of land in the Green Belt would become a double-edged sword during the post-war expansion of local authority house building, where local authority land was earmarked for large-scale development.

Winnats Pass Road, 1939

A proposal by Derbyshire County Council to construct a graded motor road through the Winnats was defeated at a public inquiry in July 1939 at which the late Joseph Husband, Professor of Civil Engineering of Sheffield University and a member of our Executive Committee, gave conclusive evidence on our behalf. In 1943, with the assistance of a legacy from Miss Ethel Marples, we were able to raise funds for the purchase of the Winnats and Mam Tor for the National Trust.

Source: *Account of Sixty-Six Years' Work 1924 to 1989.*

Edale Steelworks, 1939

Copyright Peter McDermott and licensed for reuse under a Creative Commons Licence.

CPRE Peak District and South Yorkshire's campaign against a steelworks in Edale reached the heart of Parliamentary democracy and the UK government. The campaign methods can be seen in the lively exchanges recorded in Hansard, the official report of Parliamentary debates, over two months in the summer of 1939. They can be read online.

In May 1939, Sheffield firm Brown Bayley Ltd planned to buy 50 acres at Edale Mill to make steel for RAF planes. The order came from the Air Ministry in the lead-up to the Second World War.

CPRE Peak District and South Yorkshire campaigned against the plans on several fronts. When the branch discovered the plans they wrote in the 1940 annual report that this would lead to 'the ruin of heart of the Peak, and thereby the Peak itself.' The branch orchestrated a massive letter writing campaign to the authority, Chapel-en-le-Frith Rural District Council, and regional newspapers. The planning authority agreed in principle to the development on the 1st of May 1939. and newspapers reported that building work had begun.

CPRE Peak District and South Yorkshire stepped up the campaign. They lobbied the firm to choose an alternative site and contacted MPs. 200 MPs signed a petition against the plans, wrote letters to the press and had the proposal discussed in Parliament.

MPs questioned the Secretary of State for Air and the Minister of Health in the House of Commons. MPs used powerful language. They did not want government grants used to 'destroy one of the most beautiful places in this country' and highlighted 'strong indignation in the Midlands against this vandalistic proposal.' They argued that the steelworks would ruin Edale's tourism business, create an eyesore, damage farmland, attract bombers to a designated evacuee area and lead to unemployment when closed. The two ministers initially said they were bound by planning permission granted under the Town and Country Planning Act of 1932. They quickly backtracked and agreed to speak to Brown Bayley to find an alternative site. The Minister of Health stated he was aware of CPRE's work. By July the proposal had been abandoned.

Source: *Campaign papers.*

5 The Fight for Sheffield's Green Belt
By Marianne Morgan

A view across the Rivelin Valley to the old Edward VII hospital in the trees, thankfully without an opencast coal mine above it.

The fight to create and keep the green belt around Sheffield has been going on for nearly one hundred years.

In 1937 CPRE Peak District and South Yorkshire surveyed land around Sheffield and submitted their plan for a green belt. In 1938 their proposal was accepted by Sheffield Corporation. In the north, south, east and west - farms, woods and moorland were ear-marked for the Sheffield Green Belt.

In the 1930s people could go by bus into the Peak District or escape the smoky city by walking from town to green spaces. In the 2020 COVID lockdown, many people discovered, perhaps for the first time, that having a green belt meant they could get out of the house for some exercise and enjoy walking on the moors, along our river valleys and through woods. But it could have been so different. Throughout its history, the CPRE Peak District and South Yorkshire has campaigned against the development of houses, factories and opencast mines in unsuitable places in the green belt. Thanks to their efforts we can still enjoy the many areas around our city that they protected.

How Did It Start?

In 1927 the Duke of Rutland sold Blacka Moor to a developer. To save this special place from development Alderman J.G. Graves bought it, and in 1933 gifted it to the people of Sheffield. Then in 1935 a builder bought the land between Whirlow Bridge and Dore Moor Inn to build 900 houses.

Ethel Gallimore (as she was then) told the Sheffield City Planning Committee of her idea to keep this area as a green 'Gateway to Derbyshire'. She lobbied the Council to buy the land from the developer. It also bought the Burbage and Houndkirk Moors for a water catchment area. By 1936 it owned much of the land to the west.

Ethel directly approached the Graves Trust and T. Walter Hall to buy further threatened land which they then gave to the city. Thanks to their generosity areas such as the Porter, Mayfield, Rivelin and Limb Valleys and Ryecroft Glen were protected.

Ethel and Gerald Haythornthwaite were invited to survey green belt land by Sheffield Corporation. They presented their findings, together with this map, to the Town Planning Advisory Committee in 1937. CPRE Peak District and South Yorkshire's recommendations were approved in 1938.

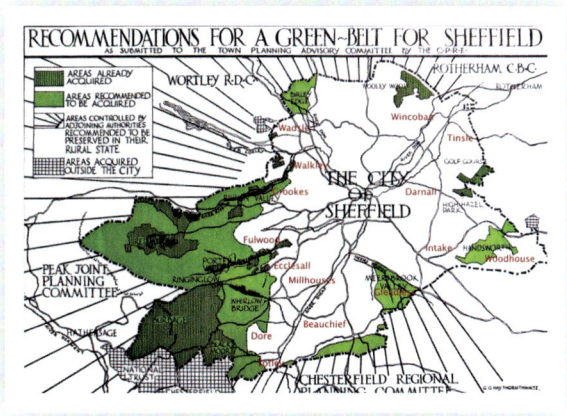

Sheffield Corporation showed much foresight and bought agricultural land, farms, woodland and moorland for the Green Belt. They even bought

The Fight for Sheffield's Green Belt | 27

land south of Norton outside the city boundary so that the Green Belt in the east would link together with the Green Belt in the west. It's hard to think of it now but it was seen as important to have farms close by to provide fresh milk and food for the people who lived in the city.

By the end of 1945, nearly all the land in the proposed Green Belt Plan of 1938 had been secured.

What Came Next?

After the war, there was an effort to clear Sheffield's slums and build new houses. The National Coal Board wanted to have an opencast coal mine near the Edward VII hospital, a steel works wanted to build in the Loxley Valley and sites were needed for refuse tips. The fight was on to stop all these threats to the Green Belt. CPRE Peak District and South Yorkshire became involved in many campaigns and the hard work began to keep it all safe.

CPRE Peak District and South Yorkshire Campaign poster, courtesy of Totley History Group.

Ethel and Gerald worked tirelessly to keep the Green Belt. The first campaign after the war was in 1946 where they successfully stopped house building on the moors above Totley, a place which was to feature in further CPRE Peak District and South Yorkshire campaigns.

In 1950, a public inquiry into a plan to build an estate at Greenhill and Bradway failed to get approval. The Minister for Housing refused permission as it would be right next to the Derbyshire Green Belt without a gap. Sheffield said it would run out of land to build houses in two years, which made Derbyshire worried that Sheffield had its eye on Dronfield!

In the end, a housing estate was planned for Mosborough, then in Derbyshire, which wasn't in a green belt. In 1962 the Boundary Commission announced changes to Sheffield's boundary that would include Mosborough. CPRE Peak District and South Yorkshire and Derbyshire CPRE had a joint campaign in 1982 because the Moss Valley had been left out of the Green Belt and the people of Killamarsh demonstrated outside the House of Commons because their valley had been left out too.

The public inquiry in 1964 into planning applications for housing in the Rivelin Valley and at Stannington was a major event. CPRE Peak District and South Yorkshire encouraged people to attend and object. They even issued a leaflet that told people which buses to catch to Stannington from town and many people raised their objections. The application to build was opposed by West Riding County Council and CPRE Peak District and South Yorkshire. Gerald Haythornthwaite put the case against with a 22-page statement. Even a 15-year-old schoolgirl from Stannington spoke against the plan. Green belt land was saved in the Rivelin Valley, but the Minister of Housing ruled in favour of building at Stannington.

A view across Rivelin Valley with a glimpse of one of the skyscrapers built at Stannington after the inquiry.

So many people turned up to the Loxley Valley public inquiry in 1975 at the Town Hall that it had to be moved from a conference room to the council chamber. The planning application was for a factory and housing. Sheffield

Council had already turned it down and CPRE Peak District and South Yorkshire also objected. In the end, the government minister ruled that the houses could not be built. However, the factory got planning permission but with certain conditions.

Throughout the years there were many campaigns – some were for small pockets of green belt others more substantial. Some places, such as Ryecroft Farm, came under threat time after time. There was a continual battle to save Whirlow Hall Farm and a campaign against building a £150 million leisure complex on the historic Oakes Park at Norton. Today both places continue to serve a useful purpose for our community.

The Green Belt Today

The fight goes on! As recently as 2021, CPRE Peak District and South Yorkshire and Loxley Valley residents won a major public inquiry, defeating a major housing development on the Hepworth's factory site. In the past town planners thought it was just about stopping cities from spreading out or providing the 'lungs of the city'. Today we know that it is also about preserving the landscape for nature and helping us all with our well-being.

In Remembrance of All Their Work

Just opposite Dore Moor Inn, at a place saved by the 1936 Whirlow Bridge to Dore Moor campaign, there stands a small wood. It was planted by CPRE Peak District and South Yorkshire and dedicated to Ethel and Gerald in honour of their lifetimes' work.

And What of the Future?

Sheffield is required to build 55,000 new houses by 2039 and CPRE Peak District and South Yorkshire is campaigning to protect Sheffield's Green Belt. Up to 11,000 of those new homes could be built in the Sheffield Green Belt, affecting communities all around the city, from Burncross to Stannington, Fulwood to Dore and Norton to Beighton.

If we want to continue to enjoy the countryside on our doorstep, we all need to support the CPRE Peak District and South Yorkshire's green belt campaign. They want future developments to be on brownfield sites in Sheffield. That way we can enjoy our green spaces and have a city designed so that it works for all of us. We haven't lost the Green Belt yet, but the work of Ethel and Gerald Haythornthwaite goes on.

6 | The Birth of National Parks - 1944-1953

Stanage Edge is one of the Peak District's beautiful and popular locations, within easy reach of Sheffield.

The Situation

Comprehensive planning and largely unfettered powers for control of development by Counties and County Boroughs were introduced by the Town and Country Planning Act 1947. Special protection and public enjoyment of the more dramatically beautiful parts of England and Wales was provided by the National Parks Act 1949, largely following the recommendations of the National Parks (Hobhouse) Committee of which both our President, Lord Chorley, and our Honorary Secretary, Mrs E.M.B. Haythornthwaite, were members.

During this period we sought:

- To ensure that the new planning powers were fully exercised to protect the Sheffield Provisional green belt and the Peak District National Park.

- To inform the public of the benefits of the Sheffield Green Belt and the Peak District National Park and secure public support for their protection.

- To encourage a better relationship between farmers in the Peak District and visitors from the towns.

Source: *Account of Sixty-Six Years' Work 1924 to 1989.*

Some of our Achievements and Campaigns

Publications

1945 *Sheffield's Green Belt.*
1945 *The Peak District a National Park.*
1947 *Town Trees.*
1950 *The Effect of the Quarrying Industry on the Scenery of the Peak District National Park.*

Green Belt Protection

Damaging development successfully resisted

Residential development:
1944 Fulwood Hall, speculative development of 18 acres.

Opencast coal working:
1951 The Moss Valley, Hazelhurst Farm and Delves Wood.
1951 The Cordwell Valley, Barlow Woodseats, Johnnygate, Cowley Hall and Barlow Highfields.
1954 The Rivelin Valley, land between King Edward VII Hospital and Stannington.

Airfields:
1951 Redmires/Lodge Moor.

Overhead electricity lines:
1949 132 kV line from Staythorpe to Oughtibridge traversing the entire green belt south, west and north of the City of Sheffield.

National Park Protection

Damaging development successfully resisted

Military uses:
1946 Leash Fen and Burbage Valley, ammunition disposal.
1947 Burbage Valley, military training area.

Opencast coal working:
1947 Lyme Handley, Lyme Park.
1949 Lyme Handley, Sponds Fields.
1949 Three Shires Head, Orchard Common.

Water supply reservoirs:
1947 The Manifold Valley, 950 acre reservoir.

Mineral extraction and processing:
1950 Doveholes, proposed cement works.
1950 Hammerton Hill, Millers Dale, proposed limestone quarry.
1950 Woo Dale and Wye Dale escarpments excluded from the extension of ICI's Tunstead Quarry.
1952 Gautries Hill, Cotterhole and Hand Dale, proposed limestone quarries.

Developments revised following our recommendations

1948 New railway tunnel, Woodhead/Dunford Bridge, tunnel portals and extension to Dunford Bridge built in local stone.
1950 Holmes Moss television station was built in local stone.

Organisational Activity

1947 Sheep rescue parties in heavy winter snows.
1950 Formation of CPRE Peak District and South Yorkshire/Ramblers/ Farmers Committee to study and resolve common problems.
1950 Formation of Peak District Stone Committee to encourage the use of stone for building in the Peak District.
1952/58 Working parties of ramblers, scouts and mountaineers to assist farmers and for litter collection.

Source: *Account of Sixty-Six Years' Work 1924 to 1989.*

How We Made a Difference

Britain's National Parks, 1945-51

The branch had campaigned to designate the Peak District as a national park since the early 1930s. This was the decade their work came to fruition, not only locally but for England and Wales. Two members of the branch were central to the work of the post-war governmental National Parks Committee - Ethel Haythornthwaite and President Lord Chorley. Their

work led to the National Parks and Access to the Countryside Act 1949. This proposed 12 national parks in England and Wales, 10 of which were designated in the 1950s.

In 1951, the Peak District was the first national park to be designated, its boundary almost identical to the one drawn by Ethel and Gerald Haythornthwaite in 1939. The Lake District, Snowdonia and Dartmoor followed later the same year, with the Pembrokeshire Coast, North York Moors, Yorkshire Dales, Exmoor, Northumberland and Brecon Beacons all being designated by the end of the 1950s. The remaining two, the New Forest and South Downs, were created in 2005 and 2009 respectively.

Davie Limestone Blocks, 1950

The use of Davie limestone blocks in Bakewell (see photo) by Mr Arnold Lowcock, ARIBA, and in many other buildings throughout the limestone area of the Peak National Park including examples shown below, has maintained the local building tradition and ensured coherent development in the limestone villages of the Peak District. The Davie block and its method of fabrication

were devised by Captain H.B. Davie-Thornhill at his Holme Bank Quarry in Bakewell in response to the promptings of our Peak District Stone Committee, of which he was a member. The Committee, which we formed in 1950 to encourage the use of stone for building in the Peak District, comprised architects, quarry owners, builders and both local and regional planning officers.

Source: *Account of Sixty-Six Years' Work 1924 to 1989.*

Manifold Valley Reservoir, 1947

In 1946 Leicester Corporation introduced a Private Bill to the House of Lords to construct a reservoir in the upper Manifold Valley with a dam 1,800 feet (550 metres) long and a maximum height of 110 feet (33 metres) below Brund and Wiggenstall which would have flooded 950 acres of excellent farmland including 23 farmsteads. Acting for the Voluntary Joint Committee for the Peak National Park we petitioned, together with the National Trust, against the Bill. After eight days proceedings, the House of Lords Select Committee rejected the Bill on 13th May 1946.

Source: *Account of Sixty-Six Years' Work 1924 to 1989.*

Above: Manifold Valley then and in 2007. Left: Copyright Stephen Henley and licensed for reuse under a Creative Commons Licence.

7 | Growth Gathers No Moss - 1954-1963

Long Dale in the Dove Valley, which was nearly turned into a motor racing track.

The Situation

The powers for planning and control of development were reinforced by the opportunity provided for the formal designation of green belts by the Ministry of Housing and Local Government Circular 42/55. Militating against the objects of planning was the undue haste to solve economic and social problems without any coordinated regional land planning policies and a distrust in the higher echelons of Government of outward beauty as a determining factor in planning practice, *"outward beauty must be seen in its proper place as one of several different elements of value to be achieved by planning and not necessarily as the dominant element."* (Page 20, para. 70 - Ministry of Town and Country Planning, Report on the Qualifications of Planners.)

National parks were given no over-riding protection by the government against damaging development and were starved of funds. Local interest in development inimical to the purposes of national parks was in some cases allowed to prevail and attempts were made to promote bizarre and damaging facilities for recreation.

Throughout this period we were continuously engaged in making representations at public inquiries or to government departments and disseminating technical information with a view to:

- Preserving and achieving formal designation for Sheffield's Provisional Green Belt and promoting a comprehensively planned dispersal of Sheffield's overspill.

- Ensuring a faithful pursuit of the purposes of national parks in the Peak District.

- Encouraging a higher standard of development control generally.

- Advancing new technology to overcome the destructive effects of reservoirs, overhead electricity transmission and domestic refuse disposal.

Source: *Account of Sixty-Six Years' Work 1924 to 1989.*

Some of our Achievements and Campaigns

Publications
1955   *A New Sheffield*, to promote planned overspill of the city.
1962   *Progress in Refuse Disposal.*

Green Belt Protection

Damaging development successfully resisted

Residential development:
1959   Middlewood, 20 acres excluded from Sheffield Corporation's housing scheme.

Helicopter Site:
1962   Redmires/Lodge Moor, proposed by Sheffield City Council.

National Park Protection

Damaging development successfully resisted

1955   200mph road racing circuit from Newhaven to Endmoor, north of Hartington, proposed by Derbyshire County Council.
1955   Moorland viewpoint pavilion and car park on Baslow Edge near Eagle Stone, proposed by the Peak Park Planning Board.
1957   Manifold walkers track - proposed Order by Staffordshire County Council authorising use by motor vehicles.
1960   50 acre domestic refuse tip at Brown Edge, Ringinglow, proposed by Sheffield City Council.
1961   Clear felling of 9 acres of Holme Wood, Stoke Hall.
1961   Airfield for light aircraft, Stanley Moor Farm, Foolow.
1961   Limestone screening and processing plant, Prospect Quarry, Via Gellia.
1963   400 kV overhead electricity line from Woodhead to Dunford Bridge.

Preservation of buildings of architectural and historic interest

1959   17th century Derwent Packhorse Bridge, re-erected on a new site at Slippery Stones in Derwent Valley.

How We Made a Difference

Hartington Racing Track, 1955

On 4th May 1955, Derbyshire County Council approved in principle a road racing circuit north of Hartington 12 miles long from Newhaven to Endmoor along the Buxton/Ashbourne Road and returning via Long and Hand Dales to complete the circuit.

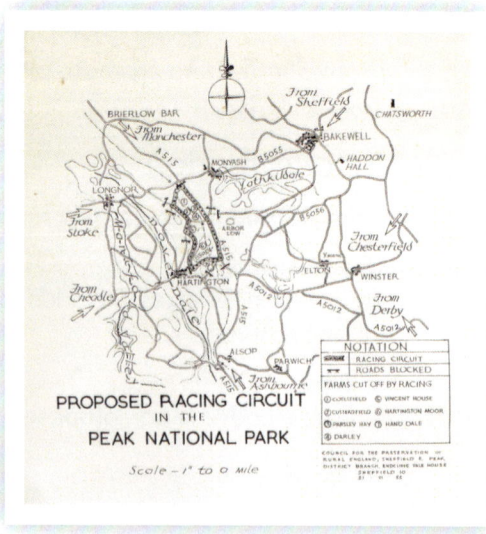

The development of the proposal envisaged the provision of parking for 25,000 visitors' cars; pits and grandstands; lavatories and sewage disposal works as well as the widening and safety fencing of the country lanes through Long Dale and Hand Dale and the erection of concrete protective walls adjacent to farmsteads along the route.

This was done unilaterally by Derbyshire County Council without consultation with the Planning Authority, the Peak Park Planning Board, of which the County Council was a constituent authority. To promote the project, it was necessary for the County Council to introduce a Private Bill in Parliament. We gave the proposal, which was in every respect contrary to the purposes of a national park, the widest publicity and were able to record in our Annual Report for 1956 that *"in the course of our many fights we have rarely stirred such a volume of national controversy."* The press were of the greatest assistance and The Times published our photographs and a leading article ending with the conclusion that *"The preservation of open spaces as valuable as the Peak District should not be tampered with to make a speed merchant's holiday."* The weight of objections nationally including Parliament, the Church and the Councils of the cities and boroughs surrounding the Peak obliged Derbyshire County Council in January 1956 to postpone the project. The fearful accident at Le Mans 200 mph circuit on 11th June 1955 in which 80 spectators in the grandstand were killed may have influenced this decision.

"It is dormant not dead" said the Council's Chairman - and so it remains after 33 years.

Source: *Account of Sixty-Six Years' Work 1924 to 1989.*

A New Sheffield, 1955

"The Green Belt is a limited amount of farmland and woodland which is rapidly being reduced by peripheral extension of the town."

Gerald Haythornthwaite had a plan to prevent Sheffield's massive growth in post-war housing being built on the Green Belt. It was a new town to the east of the city.

Gerald originally published his plan in the *Town and Country Planning Journal*, whose readership would have been the planners responsible for making decisions about post-war development. The branch reprinted this for wider circulation. This was all about influencing local authority policy and decision-making directly and by raising public awareness.

He argued that Sheffield's Green Belt was not a large area given the city's population and that a minimum area required to provide access to open countryside should be calculated. The Minister of Housing and Local Government asked local authorities to submit proposals for green belts and he expected the West Riding (now West Yorkshire) to plan to receive some of Sheffield's growing population.

Gerald's solution to avoid building on the Green Belt was bold and logical. New Sheffield could be built to the east near good rail and road networks. Steelworks could be relocated or finishing works established there, arguing that steelmaking no longer relied on the water power that led to the development of Sheffield in river valleys near the Pennines. He floated Gainsborough as an ideal location, 35 miles to the east and near the 'Great North Road.' This is the route of the A1 and was the main north-south road in the east of England before the motorways. Gerald's vision came to pass with the creation of the eastern townships, such as Mosborough.

Ringinglow Refuse Tip, 1960

Brown Edge then and in 2021. Right: Copyright Mike Penningtonand licensed for reuse under a Creative Commons Licence.

Sheffield Corporation proposed to site a 50 acre domestic refuse tip at Brown Edge in an old shallow slate pit. The site was in the Peak District National Park at 1,300 feet (395 metres) above sea level and subject to high winds and lay at the head of the Porter Clough, the culmination of the famous Sheffield City Round Walk and the main walker's route from the city into the national park. Refuse lorries making 80 journeys per day to and from the site would pass along Ringinglow Road.

This was an unbelievable proposal by Sheffield Corporation, which had done so much to ensure the preservation of the Mayfield Valley and the Porter

Clough and to make them accessible for the enjoyment of the inhabitants of Sheffield. Sheffield Corporation also was a constituent authority of the Peak District National Park, nevertheless, they appealed against the refusal of planning permission by the Peak Park Planning Board.

At the public inquiry in 1960, we supported the Planning Board and were able to provide supplementary evidence of the great effort which had been made by Sheffield Corporation themselves to protect the area and provide public access to it. The Minister dismissed the appeal stating that on amenity grounds there was an overwhelming case against it.

Source: *Account of Sixty-Six Years' Work 1924 to 1989.*

Dunford Bridge Pylons, 1963

In 1963 the Central Electricity Generating Board applied to erect a 400 kV overhead electricity line across the Woodhead Pass.

In the CEGB Newsletter No. 82, the following laconic account sums up one of the most enlightened decisions of a Government Minister - Mr Errol being the responsible Minister.

"The Peak Park Planning Board, the Council for the Preservation of Rural England and the Ramblers' Association objected to a portion of the proposed route on Pikenaze Moor, notwithstanding the CEGB's intention to remove an existing nearby 132,000 volt line. Accordingly, a public inquiry was held at Barnsley in the Autumn of 1963 and the Minister subsequently refused to sanction the proposed section of overhead line between Dunford Bridge and Woodhead. The Minister consented to a temporary

line, however, in respect of the urgency in reinforcing the supply of electricity across the Pennines."

In the following five years, the line was placed underground in the disused steam railway tunnel. The temporary overhead line shown above disfiguring the moors above Dunford Bridge remained until October 1969 and was then dismantled.

The CEGB's Newsletter No. 82 records *"Over five years of care, ingenuity and skill and nearly £2,750,000 have been spent to preserve the rugged landscape between Woodhead and Dunford Bridge."*

Source: *Account of Sixty-Six Years' Work 1924 to 1989.*

8 | Shaping Post-War Planning Policy
By Charles MacDonald-Jones

Stannington above the Rivelin Valley. Copyright Dave Pickersgill and licensed for reuse under a Creative Commons Licence.

During the Second World War, the National CPRE campaigned to protect the rural environment from post-war industrialisation.

The National CPRE wanted to influence the Committee on Land Utilisation in Rural Areas, a parliamentary committee which would influence a proposed planning act. This act would help legislate what rural land could be used for. The National CPRE influenced the act by submitting evidence to the committee, to prevent the widespread industrialisation of the countryside.

Codifying Rural Planning Policy

The Committee on Land Utilisation in Rural Areas was set up in 1941 as a parliamentary committee tasked with deciding how best to use rural land. Previous planning acts had focused on urban areas. The government hoped that a new planning act could provide a planning framework for rural areas. The committee's recommendations would be laid out in a report that would be key in developing the act.

In autumn of the same year, CPRE Peak District and South Yorkshire submitted evidence to this committee to try and influence its recommendations. CPRE

Peak District and South Yorkshire argued that the Peak District's scenery was under threat, most notably by the rapid increase of lime and cement works in the region.

The charity saw this as a crucial time for the future of the Peak District, as the recommendations of the committee, designed to be implemented after the war, could shape planning regulations for decades to come. CPRE Peak District and South Yorkshire presented its own recommendations for how rural areas should be protected by the planning system and asked its members to lobby the committee by writing letters. Evidence was requested in October 1941, but letter-writing by Ethel Haythornthwaite continued well into 1942 until the committee's Scott Report was published in August. The final contents of the report were remarkably similar to CPRE Peak District and South Yorkshire's recommendations.

The Campaign Against Industry

CPRE Peak District and South Yorkshire told the committee that, *"the introduction of industrial concerns of any size in the Peak would be injurious to sound rural life as well as a mortal blow to scenery."* In no uncertain terms, CPRE Peak District and South Yorkshire were - apart from industries associated with agriculture and tourism - against industrialisation in rural areas.

The Scott Report, named after the committee's chairman, Lord Justice Scott, seemed to largely agree with the CPRE Peak District and South Yorkshire's assessment. One recommendation suggested to keep new industry to vacant or derelict sites in towns, and that *"where industries are brought into country areas they should be located in existing or new small towns and not in villages or the open country."*

Planning for the Future

By influencing the report, CPRE Peak District and South Yorkshire hoped to shape the future of planning policy for rural areas. The Scott Report would contain recommendations to be implemented by the government. If the report was in line with the aims of CPRE Peak District and South Yorkshire, then any planning acts that followed would be more likely to enshrine protections for the countryside in law. At the time, this was not the case. The previous Town and Country Planning Act of 1932 focused on urban areas and offered no protection to much rural land.

Because of this, CPRE Peak District and South Yorkshire believed that it was an important time for the future of the Peak District and other rural areas, and that a change in planning policy was necessary to halt the rapid growth of lime and cement works and other industries. While there was a relative lack of development because of the war, there was a worry that industrial rural development could expand dramatically post-war due to a lack of protection.

Local Influence on a National Scale

This concern appears in the letters of Ethel Haythornthwaite. Correspondence between Ethel and the General Secretary of the National CPRE, H.G. Griffin, in late 1941 showed how much the National CPRE valued Ethel's input, requesting her expertise of the Peak local area: *"I am especially anxious to have a memorandum from the Peak District,"* wrote the General Secretary. Ethel contributed significantly to the charity's evidence to the committee.

She provided her own local expertise and persistent determination. Even after the evidence had been submitted, Ethel continued to write letters to the committee's secretaries, highlighting the need for national parks and other countryside developments; problems faced pre-war that were likely to return and the opposition of large-scale industries in the Peak District. In February 1942, Ethel was invited to meet with the secretaries of the Committee in London, contributing further evidence from the Peak District area.

The Minority Report for Industry

Not everyone was as convinced by the CPRE's efforts. The minority report which accompanied the Scott Report maintained that industry could be of benefit to rural communities, bringing employment, higher wages and technological advancements to the area. It was noted by both the *Manchester Guardian* and *The Times* that these observations were little considered in the Scott Report, which seemed to agree with the CPRE and Ethel.

Town and Country Planning

But the minority report was not enough to influence the government, and in 1943 the Town and Country Planning Interim Development Act was introduced. The Act, drawing on the recommendations of the previous year's Scott Report, was a success for the CPRE.

Reflecting on these changes in the mid-1950s, Gerald Haythornthwaite stated in his Notes on 'Outrage' that the Town and Country Planning Interim

Development Act of 1943, *"extended the application of planning powers to all land throughout the country."*

Planning had been essentially local, with no planning regulations to guide local authorities in rural areas. A local letter in *High Peak News* in July 1943 suggested that until that time, countryside protection had often not been a priority for many District Councils, with CPRE Peak District and South Yorkshire directly campaigning on certain local issues. Discussing Bakewell Rural District Council's decision not to build new houses in the area, local resident John Barnes said: *"I for one am devoutly thankful that our interests in this matter are being so keenly watched by our local branch of the CPRE."* With the implementation of the Town and Country Planning Interim Development Act, planning powers shaped in part by the CPRE would ensure at least some protections for every rural area.

A 1978 article by Andrew W. Gilg calling for a new 'Scott' inquiry shows the impact of the campaign. Andrew notes the success of the Scott Report, as many of its major policy recommendations have been accepted and implemented in the post-War period in four of the report's five key recommendations: the lack of industry and commerce in countryside; the poor state of agriculture; the poor state of village social life; need to preserve local amenities recognised. He did however lament the lack of overall planning direction.

Planning Today

There have been many attempts to shape an overall planning direction since the Scott Report, including in 2012 the government's National Planning Policy Framework (NPPF), which was met with widespread criticism. CPRE Peak District and South Yorkshire believed that the NPPF would place all of our countryside – including the Peak District National Park – under increasing threat, stated that the proposed framework *"places the countryside under increasing threat and leaves local communities and planning authorities largely powerless in the face of developer pressure."*

However, although the initial proposals were dropped, the NPPF is now a central part of the planning landscape, though still controversial for overriding local democracy. In many letters and speeches throughout the 20th century, Gerald Haythornthwaite declared that participation in planning and opportunity for public discussion should be encouraged. Echoing Gerald's words, ministers have promised any new reforms will have *"effective local engagement at its heart."* To ensure this is the case, we need to keep pressure on the government of the day. Perhaps the Scott Report can set an example for how that can happen?

9 | Progress Under Assault 1964-1973

Rivelin Valley from Bell Hagg. Copyright Martin Speck and licensed for reuse under a Creative Commons Licence.

The Situation

This was a period of planning confusion during which planning powers and public participation in the planning processes were both reinforced and obstructed by three Acts of Parliament:

- The Town and Country Planning Act 1971.
- The Countryside Act 1968.
- The Local Government Act 1972.

The national status of national parks suffered derogation, i.e. the weakening of protection through amended legislation, though the government undertook the greater part of the financial burden of their administration and management.

The National Parks Policy Review Committee published a report recommending far-sighted recognition of the ethos of national parks and improvement in their planning and management. (Editor: This was submitted in 1973 and published in 1974).

The greatest advance in the protection of both town and country was the preservation of buildings of architectural and historic interest and their settings as Conservation Areas.

Concurrent with this confused state of planning there were proposals for massive development of building and engineering works deep into the countryside including national parks and green belts.

Pressure upon the Sheffield, South Yorkshire and Derbyshire green belts was relieved by the allocation of 5,050 acres of land centred on Mosborough for the comprehensively planned development of Sheffield's overspill. Nevertheless, proposals have been made by Sheffield Corporation to use green belt land for residential purposes.

During this period we have worked to maintain the integrity of the countryside within the statutorily protected areas - the green belts and the Peak District National Park by:

- Winning public support for our objectives with exhibitions, lectures, broadcasts by radio and television, publications and by articles to the press.
- Monitoring planning applications, submitting recommendations to the Planning Authorities and giving evidence at public inquiries.

Our Technical Adviser and members of our Executive have served on the following Public Bodies:

- The Peak Park Planning Board.
- The Yorkshire & Humberside Economic Planning Council.
- Sheffield City Council's Conservation Advisory Group.

- Sheffield City Council's Woodlands Advisory Committee.
- Derbyshire County Council's Countryside Advisory Committee.
- Derbyshire Historic Buildings Trust Limited.

Source: *Account of Sixty-Six Years' Work 1924 to 1989.*

Some of our Achievements and Campaigns

Publications

1969   *What Price Water?*
1973   *Road Traffic in National Parks*, J. L. Womersley, CBE.

Exhibitions

1966   *CPRE in Sheffield and the Peak District.* Shown at Buxton Pavilion Gardens, Sheffield City Library and Sheffield University.

Green Belt Protection

Damaging development successfully resisted

Residential development proposed by Sheffield City Council:
1964   Rivelin Valley, 157 acres excluded from the housing scheme.
1968   Ryecroft Farm, 75 acres proposed for sale for residential development.

Speculative development:
1972   Aston, Church Lane, 45 acres.
1973   Fulwood, Sheffield, Brookhouse Hill, 5 acres.

Miscellaneous development:
1965   Redmires/Lodge Moor, 66 acre domestic refuse tip proposed by Sheffield Corporation.
1966   Rivelin Valley, Bell Hagg, 56 bedroom hotel and casino.

Buildings of architectural and historic interest protected

1972   Hellaby Hall, near Maltby.
1972   Manor House, Firbeck.

Design and choice of materials for new buildings improved

1972   Housing estate, Firbeck, Kingswood Close.

National Park Protection

Damaging development successfully resisted

Residential development for the commuter market:
1972   Bamford, near the Rising Sun Inn, 6 acres.

Reservoirs:
1970   Manifold Valley, Brund (repeat of a proposal rejected in 1947).
1970   Hassop, near Bakewell, regulating reservoir.

Mineral Workings:
1968   Hope Valley, an extension of clay workings for APCM cement works.
1970   Bradwell, extension of Outlands Head Quarry.
1970   Bradfield, Delph Road, opencast fireclay working.

Buildings of architectural and historic interest restored

1965   16th Century North Lees Hall, Outseats, Hathersage.
1968   Two cottages in Court Lane, Ashford in the Water.

How We Made a Difference

Preserving Sheffield's Green Belt, 1964 and 1971

Rivelin Valley

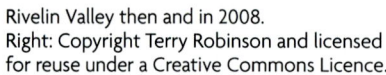

Rivelin Valley then and in 2008.
Right: Copyright Terry Robinson and licensed for reuse under a Creative Commons Licence.

A proposal by Sheffield Corporation to extend their housing scheme over 157 acres of the northern slopes of the Rivelin Valley was the subject of a public inquiry occupying seven days in April 1964. As the result of our representations, and those of many local interests, the Minister Mr Richard Crossman refused permission on the grounds that: *"Development... would involve urban encroachment on an area of great natural beauty which, precisely because of its proximity to the city, is of special value to the people of Sheffield. He is in no doubt that his Inspector's recommendation was right and this land should remain a permanent open space along the western approach to the city."*

Source: *Account of Sixty-Six Years' Work 1924 to 1989.*

Ryecroft Farm, Dore

Sheffield Corporation acquired the 74 acres of Ryecroft Farm in 1943 as an agricultural reservation and an extension to their green belt. They asked the Minister for permission in 1970 to permit the residential development of the land and its sale to building contractors. A public inquiry was held in November 1970 at which we presented the strongest objections to the proposal. In March 1971 The Secretary of State refused permission for the development, agreeing with his Inspector's conclusions that *"There is a very strong case against this development on environmental, amenity and hardship grounds, and in its favour only the argument of expediency.*

Until it is proved that a need for residential development in Sheffield exists which cannot be satisfied on less damaging sites, such as at Mosborough, or elsewhere, the objections to residential development on the application site are heavily over-riding."
Source: *Account of Sixty-Six Years' Work 1924 to 1989.*

Quarries and the National Park, 1970

Outlands Road, Bradwell. Copyright David Dixon and licensed for reuse under a Creative Commons Licence.

Campaigning against large-scale and unsightly quarrying and opencast mining across South Yorkshire and the Peak District National Park has been a major part of CPRE Peak District and South Yorkshire work. A regular sequence of events was a quarry company planning application, refusal by the Peak Park Joint Planning Board, the company lodging an appeal with the Minister for Housing and Local Government and CPRE Peak District and South Yorkshire presenting their argument at the resulting public inquiry. Here are two successes reported in the 1970 annual report, in words that illuminate CPRE Peak District and South Yorkshire's values of the time.

Bradfield, Delph Road

We are grateful to Mr Anthony Greenwood (Minister for Housing and Local Government) for his recent verdict on the Inquiry in March 1969 into an Appeal against the refusal of the Peak Park Board to permit the winning of fireclay by surface working on land at Delph Road, High Bradfield.

Bradwell, Outlands Head Quarry

Another Inquiry, whose result was anxiously awaited, was held in July, concerning Outland Quarry above Bradwell. Following a refusal by the Peak Park Board for an extension, the owners, Hoveringham Stone Company Limited, appealed. The Inquiry lasted five days and our case was taken by Colonel Haythornthwaite. Residents of Bradwell, which is adversely affected by the quarry, turned up in force. These included seven of our members who stayed for the whole of the Inquiry. The verdict, in April, by which the Minister refused the application for extension, has given neat satisfaction in the region and is significant in upholding the true values of the national parks.

Source: *CPRE Sheffield and Peak District branch Annual Report, April 1970.*

10 | A National Park Motorway 1974-1983

The Situation

This booklet was important in making the case against a motorway through Longdendale.

Much of the National Parks Policy Review Committee report of 1973 was accepted by the Department of the Environment (DoE), whose intentions to implement the recommendations were published in DoE Circular 4/76. At the same time restrictive modifications in direct contradiction of Circular 4/76 were proposed by the DoE to the Peak Park Structure Plan.

Green belts have been put at risk by the shedding of responsibility by the Secretary of State for the Environment for development which is contrary to Development Plans as promulgated in the General Development Order 1977.

As reported in our Newsletter No. 31 of January 1979 there is evidence that the Civil Service were opposed to the establishment of both national parks and green belts. The official history of Environmental Planning by Gordon E. Cherry, who had unrestricted access to Cabinet Papers and Department files, records *"The Department [of the Environment] was rarely enthusiastic about the 1949 Act [the National Parks Act] and regarded the Commission with no great warmth... it is difficult to resist the feeling that they considered the task of national parks and countryside planning as more properly theirs."*

In September 1979 a remarkable series of Topic Papers was issued by a Countryside Review Committee chaired and serviced by the Department of the Environment. Topic Paper No. 4 proposed, *inter alia*, the abolition of national parks and their replacement by a two-tier system. The top tier would consist of small areas of outstanding quality selected from within the present national parks and areas of outstanding natural beauty. This top tier would be administered nationally. The second tier would be the remainder of the national parks and areas of outstanding natural beauty managed by an executive committee composed of representatives of the local authorities concerned. Ministerially appointed representation as on present national park bodies would be eliminated.

We were obliged to comment that the reasons advanced for such destructive proposals were not only unfounded but wildly misleading. For example, that *"The appointment of Ministerial members to National Park Boards and Committees is often resented by the local authorities."* An assertion entirely contradicted by the election of Ministerial appointees as Vice Chairmen on seven of the Peak Park Planning Board's Committees.

Fortunately, the discussion paper was described by Mr Tom King, Minister for Local Government and Environment, as Civil Servants speaking from personal experience, a personal contribution with no endorsement from the Government. Nevertheless, this exercise endorses Gordon E. Cherry's opinion and finds expression in a number of disabling proposals currently in the field of Town and Country Planning such as the proposed abolition of County Structure Plans.

However, most Ministers and Secretaries of State have provided a defence against such weakening of protective legislation and our hope is that by adequate representation we may be able in general to secure the future of the countryside.

During this period we have worked to maintain the integrity of the countryside within the statutorily protected areas - the green belts and the Peak District National Park by:

- Winning public support for our objectives with exhibitions, lectures, broadcasts by radio and television, by publications and by articles to the press.

- Monitoring planning applications submitting recommendations to the Planning Authorities and giving evidence at public inquiries.

Our Technical Adviser and members of our Executive have served on the following Public Bodies:

- The Council for National Parks.
- The Peak Park Planning Board.
- The Yorkshire & Humberside Economic Planning Council.
- Sheffield City Council's Conservation Advisory Group.
- Sheffield City Council's Moorlands and Amenity Woodlands Advisory Group.
- Derbyshire County Council's Countryside Advisory Committee.
- Derbyshire Historic Buildings Trust Limited.

Source: *Account of Sixty-Six Years' Work 1924 to 1989.*

Some of our Achievements and Campaigns

Publications

1974 *A Motorway in a National Park.*

Green Belt Protection

Damaging development successfully resisted

Residential development proposed by Sheffield City Council:
1978   High Storrs, 18 acres proposed for sale for residential development.

Speculative development:
1975   Wadsley and Loxley Valley, Sheffield, 27 acres.
1975   Windmill Hill, Chapeltown, 25 acres.
1976   Loxley Valley, Sheffield, Long Lane/France Road, 25 acres.
1977   Worrall, Grenoside and Ecclesfield, 28 acres.
1979   Lognor, Lane Head, residential development on 7.5 acres.
1980   The Dale, Killamarsh, proposed a residential development comprising 1,200 houses.

1980 Wadsley, Aldene Road and Stour Lane, 15 ½ acres for residential development.
1981 Loxley, Low Matlock Road, 37 dwellings.
1982 Whiston, between Worrygoose Lane and East Bawtry Road, 110 acres of residential development.
1983 Sheffield, Middlewood Road North, residential development next to Asylum Cottages.

Sports centres and golf courses in unsuitable locations:
1977 Cutthorpe, Birley Grange Farm, golf course.
1978 Loxley, Myers Lane/Long Lane, sports centre and golf course.

Buildings of architectural and historic interest protected

1974 Albion Row Cottages, Rivelin Valley, Sheffield.
1974 Warren House, Bramley.
1974 Housely Hall, Chapeltown.

Design and choice of materials for new buildings improved

1976 Housing estate of 37 acres at Acorn Hill, Sheffield.

Extension to the Sheffield green belt

1978 Land of Whirlow Hall Farm.

National Park Protection

Damaging development successfully resisted

Residential development for the commuter market:
1975 Baslow, near the Wheatsheaf Inn, 4 ½ acres.

Miscellaneous development:
1976 Refuse tip, Rivelin Valley, Lawns Farm, operation stopped and the site restored.
1977 Motorway (M67) Sheffield to Manchester over Woodhead Pass.
1982 Wardlow, Middle Hay, motorcycle scrambling.
1983 Ashford in the Water, Riverside Hotel, timeshare apartments.
1983 Grindleford, site of a former tip, removal of low-grade fuel by road.

How We Made a Difference

Sheffield to Manchester M67 Motorway, 1977

For 12 years we campaigned to prevent a motorway across the Peak District National Park through Longdendale and over the Woodhead Pass. Our efforts were crowned in 1977 by a decision of the Secretary of State, Mr William Rodgers, announcing that *"On economic grounds, the building of a new road cannot be justified... I hope that this decision will also be welcome to those who were unhappy on environmental grounds about the building of a new road through the Peak District National Park."* Where the proposed motorway would have traversed the Etherow Basin shown in the uppermost photograph, the effect would have been utterly disastrous. An impression of the damage which would have been caused is shown in the lower photograph where the Rakewood Viaduct on the M62 has been superimposed.

Source: *Account of Sixty-Six Years' Work 1924 to 1989.*

See Chapter 11 Long and Winding Roads for how this campaign against a major road through Longdendale continues to this day.

Sheffield Green Belt Public Inquiry, 1982

The long-awaited public inquiry into the Sheffield Green Belt Plan began on 29th June 1982. It was to last until 23rd July. The Inspector, Mr D.F. Harris, MRTPI, appointed by the Secretary of State for the Environment, listened carefully and impartially to the cases for and against all the objections to Sheffield's Plan. The Inspector produced his report on the inquiry

in January 1983 and CPRE Peak District and South Yorkshire were delighted with his recommendations. Their stance over the last 45 years had been entirely vindicated. Sheffield considered the report and to CPRE Peak District and South Yorkshire's great relief, they decided to accept all 34 of the Inspector's recommendations, except for three which they accepted only in part. The Green Belt Plan was adopted as a statutory local plan at a council meeting on 30th November 1983 and became operative on 5th December 1983. The exceptional countryside around Sheffield had finally been given some degree of permanent protection, after 45 years of campaigning, until the Green Belt Review in 1996.

Source: *Account of Sixty-Six Years' Work 1924 to 1989.*

Saving Rivelin Valley Cottages, 1974

Albion Row Cottages then and in 2009. Right: Copyright Terry Robinson and licensed for reuse under a Creative Commons Licence.

Following a request by one of our members living in Albion Row, a group of 10 characteristic stone cottages at Rivelin, we sought the help of the City Planning Officer and Architect to retrieve these from a demolition order. With the Department's encouragement, we were fortunate in obtaining the interest of the Landmark Trust who were ready to purchase and re-condition the cottages. In the event, this was unnecessary, as with the assistance of the Sheffield Corporation, the demolition order was rescinded and the five sitting tenants were able to effect the reconditioning themselves.

Source: *Account of Sixty-Six Years' Work 1924 to 1989.*

Acorn Hill, Stannington, Housing Design, 1976

Acorn Hill then and in 2011.
Right: Copyright Jonathan Clitheroe and licensed for reuse under a Creative Commons Licence.

Sheffield City Council applied for and received permission from the Secretary of State to sell 37 acres of land at Acorn Hill, Stannington, which they had acquired for their own housing purposes, to private building contractors.

Permission was granted subject to a layout and design approved by the Secretary of State. The material to be used for the houses was local stone. This layout was exemplary.

In 1976, the City Council, having arranged the sale of the land to Messrs. Gleesons, sought a modification of the layout and design of the houses and the use of a substitute material for the natural stone previously approved. We objected to the Modification Order and following a public inquiry in June 1976, the Secretary of State refused to confirm the Order agreeing with the Inspector's conclusions that *"I consider the present proposals abandoned almost every feature of the approved details which would contribute to the achievement of a high standard of appearance... I consider the implementation of planning permission modified in the manner proposed would result in development very much inferior to that previously approved and of a standard unsuitable for this important site near the boundary of the National Park."*

The development now proceeding generally in accordance with the original approved layout and design is excellent and a very acceptable addition to the fine countryside surrounding it as may be seen above.

Source: *Account of Sixty-Six Years' Work 1924 to 1989.*

11 | Long and Winding Roads
By Bill Bevan

Roads and the Peak District

Traffic started to increase dramatically in the 1950s, stimulating a programme of road building that ranged from road widening and roundabouts to bypasses and major new road schemes such as the TransPennine motorway. CPRE Peak District and South Yorkshire initially campaigned to reduce the impact of road building on the beauty of the Peak District National Park. It adopted a range of campaign techniques, including letter writing, lobbying government ministers, raising public awareness, attending public enquiries, conducting traffic surveys, being part of transport committees and commenting on specific proposals. Perhaps the greatest success was to prevent the motorway from being built across the northern part of the national park. This is a campaign that continues today and opposing major road building in Longdendale and Glossopdale remains a priority.

Longshaw Estate -
Photo: G.G. Haythornthwaite

One of the many photographs taken by CPRE Peak District and South Yorkshire to highlight the problem of traffic in the Peak District. This is now Surprise View Car Park.

Why was it About Roads?

Two increases in road traffic mostly affected the Peak District. Car ownership increased five-fold between 1950 and 1970 to account for 77% of all passenger miles in the UK by 1970. Car ownership doubled again between 1970 and 2000. The use of lorries for haulage passed rail freight in the 1930s and kept on increasing by almost 6% each year. By 1970, 80% of freight was by road.

Government and councils responded to more vehicles by building more roads. The motorway system started with the M1 in 1959. Main and minor roads were improved and widened, the modern roundabout was invented, and towns were bypassed. People benefitted from better roads and car ownership with greater mobility and access to the countryside. More and more people visited the Peak District by car.

CPRE Peak District and South Yorkshire was not worried about the number of people, they saw the Peak District National Park as a place to be enjoyed by all for its peace and beauty. The issue for most of the 20th century was how new roads damaged the countryside and increased noise pollution. CPRE Peak District and South Yorkshire felt that road building should be limited in a national park.

Small Changes Driven Through

CPRE Peak District and South Yorkshire were concerned about the many small road changes that were made to accommodate greater numbers of vehicles. The county highways agencies widened roads, built concrete bridges and installed large roundabouts without needing planning permission. In 1963, Gerald, as Chair of the Standing Committee for National Parks, created a motor vehicle memorandum and sought support from the Ramblers Association, YHA, AA, RAC, and Cyclists' Touring Club.

CPRE Peak District and South Yorkshire always offered practical solutions and lobbied for the improvement of passenger and freight rail services and campaigned against the closure of two threatened TransPeak railway lines in the 1960s – Hope Valley and Woodhead lines. They helped to keep the Hope Valley Line open, but the Woodhead Line closed in the 1980s. In 1971, a new steel plant in Scunthorpe increased demand for Buxton limestone, which was carried across the Peak District by road. CPRE Peak District and South Yorkshire came up with a plan to take the limestone by lorry to the railhead at Buxton and then to Scunthorpe by train.

Campaign Tactics

Much of CPRE Peak District and South Yorkshire's work involved writing letters to government Ministers, the county highways officer and newspapers. They also surveyed traffic patterns, objected to proposals and commented on public consultations.

Gerald Haythornthwaite was in the thick of the action and wrote an article for the Institution of Highway Engineers in 1970. He argued for the development of a road system in the Peak District that would do the least harm to the countryside and benefit road users would be met by closer involvement of the highway authorities in the wider issues of planning. He covered road patterns, terrain, traffic types, future trends, deflecting traffic, motorways, A roads, minor roads, car parks and motor-less zones.

Peak Transport Policy

CPRE Peak District and South Yorkshire achieved a major goal when the National Park Authority set up a transport study in 1979. It took a park-wide strategic look at transport needs and road improvements with recommendations that included keeping the Woodhead Line open for freight, assessing whether the Snake Pass should be closed to through traffic, advising the Highways Authority that minor road schemes would not alleviate traffic problems and that traffic issues in the Park should be a multi-agency issue.

Two notable transport campaign successes for CPRE Peak District and South Yorkshire centred on Bakewell and Longdendale.

Bakewell Bypass

The plan to bypass Bakewell's town centre began in 1936 and resurfaced in 1957.

The proposal was to divert the A6 by building a wide, fast road across the water meadows by Holme Lane and the Show Ground to the northeast of the town, creating a new junction with the A619 at its junction with Coombs Road. Part of the route required a major new modern bridge. In 1936, Gerald wrote an article in *Derbyshire Countryside* magazine and had 500 copies printed as a leaflet. He described Bakewell as the kinder side of Derbyshire's nature and stated its outstanding charm was the town's relationship with its river pastures. These would be lost, as would the visitors who were attracted to the town's peace and beauty. CPRE Peak District and South Yorkshire estimated that the bypass would be of no benefit to motorists, who would only gain three minutes journey time, while the intrinsic life and charm of Bakewell would be lost. The scheme was dropped in 1937.

When the bypass was proposed again in 1957, the branch campaigned against the disfigurement of Bakewell once again and a public enquiry was held in 1969. Despite the presentation of CPRE Peak District and South Yorkshire's convincing objections by Gerald and an attorney, the National Park Authority and the government approved the scheme. It has never been implemented and would, surely, now be seen as an act of landscape vandalism.

Motorway Through Longdendale

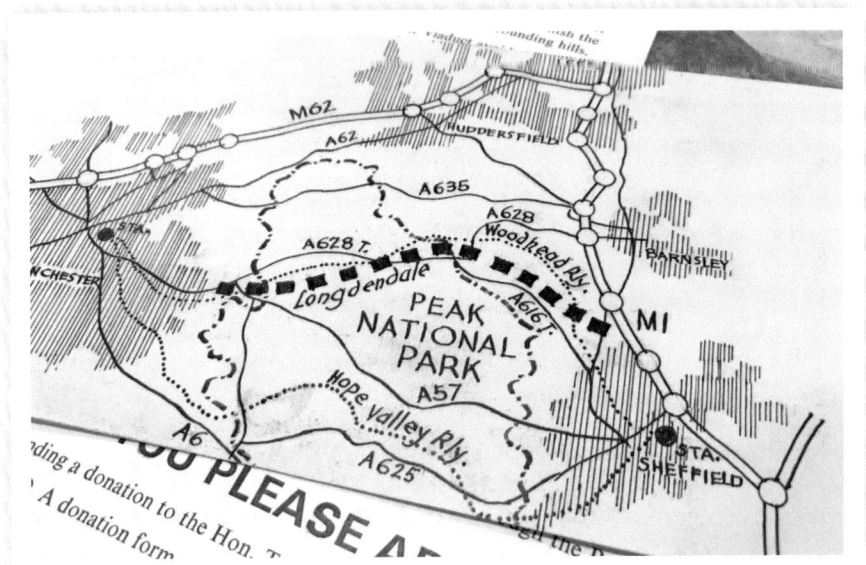

The proposal for a main road or motorway between Manchester and Sheffield through Longdendale was announced in 1972 in the House of Commons. CPRE Peak District and South Yorkshire quickly coordinated a group of organisations under the banner of The Voluntary Joint Committee for the Peak National Park to raise public opposition to the plans before the proposals went to public consultations.

They produced a booklet with photos of the M62, plans of the predicted route, a photo showing an M62 viaduct overlain in Longdendale and evocative language. They visualised a motorway similar to the M62 - a wide road, with concrete viaducts, deep cuttings, the 'alien presence' of sodium road lights 'projected into the night and the glare of the lights radiates far over the country', traffic interchanges and a maintenance slip road.

"The dominating structure of a motorway having no response to the nature of the land, disregarding its natural formation and deforming its features would diminish its natural beauty. The din, stink and feverish movement of the motorway traffic would drive out peace. A motorway therefore is wholly incompatible with the two purposes for which national parks have been established."

The booklet proposed alternatives to the motorway, to develop the Woodhead and Hope Valley railway lines. They went into technical detail about the capacity, cost-effectiveness and low-carbon benefits of the Woodhead's electrified line, including feeding energy back to the electricity grid via regenerative braking downhill. The booklet ended with an appeal for donations and urging members of societies to pass a resolution to object.

The backers of the scheme saw the benefits to Sheffield's economy as attracting new industries, reducing freight costs, and improving journey times. There were also benefits seen to taking traffic away from small towns and villages nearby and off the Snake Pass and Hope Valley Rd.

Gerald also gave talks and wrote letters to newspapers, often in response to supporters of the motorway.

The Ministry of Transport continued with a traffic survey of the route until 1977 when the proposal was scrapped 'until 2000.' The scheme was replaced with plans to improve the existing A628, including bypasses at Tintwistle,

Hollingworth and Mottram. The scheme returned in the 2000s as a dual carriageway expressway and was again opposed by CPRE Peak District and South Yorkshire and defeated at public inquiry.

Today

CPRE Peak District and South Yorkshire has a downloadable transport policy, campaigns for sustainable transport and provides practical solutions. The Hope Valley Line remains an important alternative to the car and CPRE Peak District and South Yorkshire continues to support service improvements. The branch continues to oppose new roads in Longdendale and Glossopdale.

12 | From Commercial Development to Renewable Energy - 1984-1993

The Situation

Royd Moor Windfarm.

We wish to echo Lord Seaman's opinion in *The Times* of 18th January 1990: *"the man behind the 1947 Planning Act was a hero, Silkin saved the English landscape when some European countries were losing theirs, but now the central purpose of planning and land use has lost its way. We have become overwhelmed by the volume and complexity of legislation."*

This was a time of immense developments when house building, high-tech industrial projects, huge supermarkets and equally huge car parks and road building threatened the peace and beauty of our countryside. We have sought to maintain the integrity of the countryside within the statutorily protected areas of the green belts of Sheffield and Rotherham and the Peak District National Park by:

- Monitoring planning applications submitted to Sheffield and Rotherham MBCs, the Peak Park Planning Board, the North East Derbyshire District Council and the High Peak Borough Council, and, where necessary submitting recommendations to the Planning Authorities and appearing at public inquiries in support of our recommendations.
- Seeking public support for our objectives with lectures, publications and press correspondence.

The branch published a statement on renewable energy and windfarms in the 1992 annual report. Stating that 'harnessing renewable sources for the supply of clean energy has always been a goal of environmentalists. During 1991, this dream moved closer to reality.' The branch also stated that 'Britain has the best wind regime in Europe, but the most favourable sites for windpower developments frequently coincide with our finest upland and coastal landscapes.' The first local windfarm application was made in 1991 for 13 turbines at Royd Moor, Penistone. Within a year a total of 27 applications were made, nearly all on moorland adjacent to the Peak District National Park. This was the branch position:

'The branch has committed itself to resisting the pressures for large-scale commercial development in such important landscapes. We do not accept that windpower constitutes a special case. Proposals should conform to the same requirements and constraints as other forms of development. Where the countryside has been specifically designated for its high landscape quality, this should be a primary factor in the consideration of planning applications. We have argued that windpower should be part of an overall national energy strategy, which includes energy conservation and the need to minimise the environmental effects of all forms of energy generation.'

Our officers and members of our branch have served on the following bodies:

- Council for National Parks.
- Peak Park Planning Board.
- Sheffield City Council's Conservation Advisory Group.
- Sheffield City Council's Woodlands and Moorlands Advisory Group.
- Derbyshire Historic Buildings Trust.

- Derbyshire County Council's Countryside Advisory Committee.
- Sheffield Wildlife Conservation Group.

Sources: *Account of Sixty-Six Years' Work 1924 to 1989,* Annual Reports 1990-1994.

Some of our Achievements and Campaigns

Publications, Events and Local Plan Comments

1990   Why Quarry Discussion Day in Bradwell. This brought together speakers from the National Parks, Derbyshire County Council and Blue Circle Cement to talk about long-term planning to mitigate damage and alternative sources of materials.

1990   Branch boundary expanded to include all of South Yorkshire.

1992   Peak District National Park Replacement Structure Plan, major submissions made.

1993   Unitary Development Plans for Barnsley, Doncaster, Rotherham and Sheffield, major submissions made.

1993   Bakewell Draft Interim Policy revised by Peak Park Joint Planning Board.

1993   High Peak Draft Local Plan, major response.

1993   Transport Campaign Group was founded.

Green Belt Protection

1990   Rotherham Green Belt Plan approved by the Secretary of State.

Damaging development successfully resisted:

Speculative development:

1984   Wickersley, off Second Lane, residential development.

1986   Sheffield, Manchester Road, 20 houses and garages on a former sports field.

1986   Treeton, Flatts Lane, residential development.

1987   Ravenfield, Moor Lane North, residential development.

1988   Aston cum Aughton, Aston Lane, residential development.

1989   Mosborough, Westwell Farm, residential development.

1989   Maltby, Carr Lane, Hooton Levitt, residential development.

1989   Grenoside, Skew Hill Lane, residential development.

1989   Loxley, Greaves Lane and Myers Grove Lane, residential development.

Miscellaneous development:

1985 Sheffield, Beauchief, accommodation adjacent to Beauchief Hall to form a health farm with 50 bedrooms and dining facilities.
1987 Sheffield Rivelin Valley, The Reaps, proposed caravan site, ski centre, offices, shops, cafe, chalets and car park.
1987 Norton, former RAF camp, superstore and associated car parking, petrol station and garden centre.
1987 Rotherham, Canklow Woods, 2 dry ski slopes and ancillary building.
1988 Loxley, Pine Grove Country Club, hotel with car park.
1988 Rotherham, south of West Bawtry Road and east of Long Lane. 200 bedroom hotel and conference centre.
1988 Rotherham, south of West Bawtry Road and west of Long Lane, 100 bedroom hotel including conference and banqueting facilities for Saxon Hotels.
1989 Norton, Oakes Park, 120,000 sq. ft. supermarket, car parking for 1000 cars and 300-370 housing units.
1989 Aston, adjacent to the M1 motorway, 150 bedroom hotel with restaurant, conference and leisure facilities.
1991 Rivelin Valley, water treatment works. We put forward alternative plans for design improvements. The approved application included the use of traditional materials and improved landscaping and screening.
1991 Cowdale, Buxton, Hooton Levitt and Kiveton Park, Rotherham, golf courses.
1993 Broad Carr Road, Hoyland, open cast coal mine.

National Park Protection

Damaging speculative development successfully resisted:

1989 Bakewell, Moorhall and Monyash Road, 6.6 acres.
1989 Castleton, Bean Hill Farm, 37 houses.
1989 Bakewell, River Gardens, Buxton Road, 11.4 acres

Miscellaneous development:

1984 Castleton, Winnats Pass, extraction of Blue John Stone from Old Tor Mine.
1986 King Sterndale, Topley Pike, quarry extension.
1987 Sparrowpit, Eldon Hill Quarry extension.
1988 Bakewell, Haddon Road. 'High Tech' factory including parking for 100 cars.

How We Made a Difference

60th Anniversary of the branch, 1984

1,000 trees were planted to commemorate the founding of CPRE Peak District and South Yorkshire by Mrs Ethel Gallimore (later Haythornthwaite) at Longshaw. The first trees were planted by our President, Sir Eric Mensforth. The cost was borne equally by the Countryside Commission and by our branch.

Source: *Account of Sixty-Six Years' Work 1924 to 1989.*

Eldon Hill Quarry, 1987

Eldon Hill Quarry is one of the most conspicuous eyesores in the Peak District National Park. In 1939 we approached the owners of Eldon Hill requesting that a limit should be placed on the extent of the quarry but without success. In 1952 we opposed the extension of the quarry without success, but the Minister limited the operation of the quarry to a period ending on 29th September 1997. An application to extend the quarry, to which we objected, was the subject of a further inquiry opening at Buxton on 19th November 1985. Our Assistant Technical Officer appeared on 16 days during appalling weather conditions with snow-bound roads, for which she and the branch were rewarded by the Secretary of State refusing the application on 24th February 1987.

Source: *Account of Sixty-Six Years' Work 1924 to 1989.*

Rotherham Green Belt, 1988

Whiston, Rotherham. Copyright Ryk Rak and licensed for reuse under a Creative Commons Licence.

The Inquiry into the Rotherham Green Belt Plan was held in 1988. However, major modifications were proposed by the Council which formed the subject of a further public inquiry in November 1989. The branch appeared and presented objections to the removal of two large sites at Whiston and Bramley and a smaller site at Throapham.

Source: *Account of Sixty-Six Years' Work 1924 to 1989.*

13 | New Challenges - 1994-2003

Thorne Moor after peat extraction ended in 2001.

The Situation

Work to protect green belts and the Peak District National Park from development, quarrying and roadbuilding, as well as influence building design, continued to make up a major part of the branch's work. Several major new challenges also appeared over the horizon as the decade progressed, specifically Regional Development Agencies, Objective 1 funding, mobile phone masts and the loss of hedgerows. Among all of this, a new opportunity prompted a new name.

In 1994 the branch was formally adopted as the National Park Society for the Peak National Park, under the name Friends of the Peak District.

New Regional Development Agencies have absorbed the Rural Development Commission's regeneration role but their remit seemed largely drawn from urban experience with a hard development focus. The rest of the RDC was merged with the Countryside Commission into a new Countryside Agency. Regional Development Agencies were responsible for planning land use and transport and CPRE Peak District and South Yorkshire responded by appointing Regional Policy Officers.

European Union Objective 1 funding was granted to South Yorkshire in 1999 to stimulate economic growth. Yorkshire Forward was created to manage the budget and develop a plan for strategic economic zones along the M1 and M18 corridors. The branch sought to influence how the money would be spent and the funding's rural agenda. The 2003 mid-term review of the programme highlighted that the 'implementation of the environmental sustainability cross-cutting theme had been slowest.'

Windfarms in the windy uplands continued to tax the branch during the decade. In 1994, the then existing branch policy to oppose windfarms in sensitive landscapes was maintained. By 2001 this had evolved and the branch reviewed how to respond to applications given the need to reduce damage from acid rain and climate change. By 2003, the branch supported small-scale renewable energy projects in the Peak District, such as domestic solar panels in the Bradwell Conservation Area but opposed wind turbines in prominent locations such as a large windfarm on High Edge, Buxton.

Transport continued to be a major issue. The branch monitored local authority 'Transport Policies and Programmes' documents and, from 1999, commented on regional Integrated Transport Strategies, Local Transport Plans and the inter-regional South Pennines Integrated Transport Strategy, all likely to affect local road and rail routes. The proposal to widen the A628/A616 (once the location for the proposed motorway) was put to bed by the Minister of Transport in 1994. In 2000, the proposal refused to lie down when the South Pennines Integrated Transport Strategy recommended the A628 should carry all cross-park traffic. A Mottram-Tintwistle bypass was also proposed by the Highways Agency, which the branch strongly responded to. An A628 road scheme continues to be wide awake in 2024.

Three major quarry applications either ended or began during this decade. A long-running campaign to save Eldon Hill from further quarrying finally came to fruition in 1999. However, 1996 saw limestone quarrying expand enormously at Longstone Edge under the pretence of fluorspar working. A large planning application for gritstone quarrying on Stanton Moor was submitted in 1998. The branch and local community action groups would dig deep into their time and energy on these latter two campaigns, which would run well into the 21st century.

The level of damage to the Peak District from old mineral permissions led the branch to establish the Minerals Campaign Group in 2000. Twelve committed members, including representatives from local campaign groups at Longstone Edge, Stanton Moor and Stoney Middleton, would have a lot of work to do over the next few years.

With increasing mobile phone use, phone masts became a major focus of work in response to an increasing number of planning applications across the Peak District during the late 1990s. 'Another insidious threat to the appearance of the countryside is the steady march of telecommunications masts, mostly erected by competing phone operators under the specially relaxed planning regime introduced by the previous government.' The branch supported the National CPRE, who updated its Telecommunications Briefing Notes during 1998, and local authorities, who wanted to bring proposals for masts under full planning control. 'The government has made minor amendments and several operators are following best practice guidelines, but there is still some way to go as some of our most cherished landscapes are targeted for development.' Applications for masts were opposed in Totley, Whirlow, Rivelin, Brightholmlee, Oughtibridge, Dore, and the Snake Pass. By 2002, the branch launched a 'mast-free wild areas campaign,' which had variable success.

Hedgerow loss became a major local campaign from 1997 when government introduced Hedgerow Regulations. The branch supported CPRE Peak District and South Yorkshire's national Hedgerow Campaign with a volunteer who raised public awareness of the Regulations, surveyed hedges, promoted new hedge-planting and responded to applications for hedgerow removal.

Source: *Based on Annual Reports.*

Some of our Achievements and Campaigns

Publications, Events and Local Plan Comments

1995   Peak Park Joint Planning Board, Draft Local Plan. Major comments submitted.

2000 Hedgerow Report published.
2000 Minerals Campaign Group founded.
2000 Green Travel Campaign started.
2000 Stanton Moor quarry summer event with Stanton Lees Action Group.

Green Belt Protection

Damaging development successfully resisted:

1994 Campsall limestone quarry refused.
1994 Firbeck Hall, new village residential development refused.
1995 Howbrook, opencast coal mine refused.
1995 Thorpe Hesley, Rotherham, service area and motel at M1 Junction 35 refused.
1997 Middlewood Hospital, planning brief revised.
1998 Hayfield Lane, Finningley, landfill site refused.
2000 The Warren, Rotherham, housing development refused.
2000 Thorpe Hesley, Rotherham, 1200 houses refused.
2001 Wortley, Barnsley, housing scheme withdrawn.
2001 Hatfield and Thorne Moors, peat extraction ended.
2002 Dearne Valley, Barnsley, open-cast coal mining refused.
2002 Andrew Clough, New Mills, housing development refused.
2002 North East Derbyshire, local plan amended to protect greenfield sites.

National Park Protection

1994 Minister of Transport rules out the upgrading of the A628 / A616 through the national park save in exceptional circumstances.
1995 Eldon Quarry, extension refused.
1999 Bonsall Moor, Tearsall Quarry extension refused.
1999 Alport Dale, replace conifer plantations with restoration of native woodland and bilberry moor.
2003 Watersaw Rake, Longstone, fluorspar workings refused.
2003 Upper Derwent, phone masts refused on the Snake Pass and Win Hill.
2003 High Edge, wind farm refused.

How We Made a Difference

Alport Dale

In 1995 the Forestry Commission planned to harvest trees from its high altitude conifer plantations at the top of Alport Dale above the Ashop Valley. The uniform dark unchanging colour, formal outline and stark edges of the plantations had dominated the area near Alport Castles for decades. The trees had been planted with horses. Harvesting would have required building a large road for one and a half miles along the valley to take heavy articulated lorries. The work would have been intrusive, loud and disruptive to a tranquil part of the Peak District. Once felled, the plantation was to be replanted.

A major campaign against the proposals was led by local resident Anne Robinson, who would become the branch Chair in 2002. A successful media campaign motivated 6,000 people to sign a petition and 350 people to write letters. This was against a background of cheap timber imports which had a disastrous impact on local timber production.

The result was a resounding success. Ownership of the land was passed on to the National Trust who, with the Forestry Commission, developed a long-term vision for the valley in consultation with residents, visitors, the National Park Authority and CPRE Peak District and South Yorkshire.

In what was called 'an experimental and courageous process' in 2005, the conifers are now in a forty-year cycle of small-scale felling and ring-barking to kill trees while standing up. Logs are left in place to help create new habitats. Alongside tree removal, dry-stone walls are being rebuilt and rewilding is allowed to take place to create a mosaic of native woodlands and moorlands.

Source: *Based on the 2000 Annual Report.*

Thorpe Hesley

Fields near Thorpe Hesley. Copyright Jonathan Clitheroe and licensed for reuse under a Creative Commons Licence.

A major housing development of 1,200 new houses on Rotherham's green belt would have almost doubled the size of Thorpe Hesley, a village to the north of Rotherham. The houses were planned for fields between the village and the M1 motorway near junction 35. The application was submitted around the time the government published its new planning guidance that said new houses should be built on urban brownfield sites before green fields are considered. The branch worked with the local community to oppose the development. The application went to a public inquiry where it was turned down because brownfield sites were available elsewhere in the borough.

Source: *Based on the 2000 and 2001 Annual Reports.*

14 | Digging in Against Quarries
By Bill Bevan

Eldon Hill Quarry. Copyright Neil Theasby and licensed for reuse under a Creative Commons Licence.

One of the major long-term campaigns of CPRE Peak District and South Yorkshire is against the destructive impact of large and intrusive quarries and opencast mines.

The big issues have been opencast mines in South Yorkshire and North East Derbyshire, and limestone quarries in the Peak District. The branch has campaigned against any mine or quarry that would damage the beauty and tranquillity of rural landscapes, including large-scale peat extraction. While CPRE Peak District and South Yorkshire has tried to protect local natural beauty, they have also argued against quarries because of noise, dust, traffic and, more recently, climate change.

The branch used a range of campaign techniques, from trying to influence local planning and national legislation by writing policy articles and lobbying local and national government, to leading campaigns against specific planning applications. CPRE Peak District and South Yorkshire has written letters of objection, called for public enquiries and encouraged members and other organisations to object. At different times, they have mobilised national institutions, community groups, Lords and MPs, as well as ordinary individuals.

Opencast

Opencast coal mine on the Wentworth Woodhouse Estate.

Deep and opencast coal mines have left their mark on South Yorkshire's landscape, alongside sand, gravel and limestone quarries, and peat extraction.

At different times in the past, the CPRE has preferred coal imports and nuclear to local opencast coal. Currently, no opencast coal sites operate in South Yorkshire or North East Derbyshire, and the branch campaigns against coal-fuelled power stations because of the fossil fuel's impact on climate change. Over the years, the branch successfully opposed opencast coal mines at Lyme Handley, Kettleshulme (1949), Barlow, Chesterfield (1951), Cowley Hall, Dronfield (1951), Rivelin Valley, Sheffield (1954), Hoyland, Barnsley (1993) and Howbrook, Barnsley (1995).

Several large quarries provide aggregate for road building and construction on the limestone ridge that runs north to south through Doncaster and Rotherham. Some specialist dolomite limestone quarries provide material for glass making. Doncaster also has sand and gravel pits which spread over very large areas of the countryside. When they are restored, they can provide valuable lakes and wetlands for wildlife or can be returned to agriculture.

Large-scale peat removal used to take place on the lowland peat bogs of Thorne and Hatfield Moors, but the main permissions have now been revoked.

National Park Quarries

Limestone and gritstone quarries have seen major campaigns in the Peak District National Park, starting from the year the branch was formed in 1924, before the area was designated as a national park. The region is a major source of limestone, mostly for aggregates, with many extensive and ill-defined quarry permissions awarded before the national park was established in 1951. There are also some gritstone quarries, especially clustering on and around Stanton Moor.

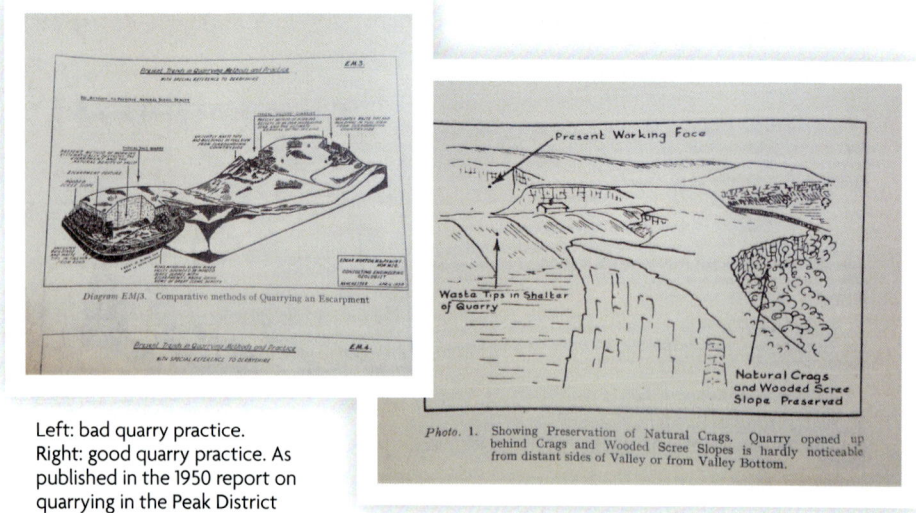

Left: bad quarry practice.
Right: good quarry practice. As published in the 1950 report on quarrying in the Peak District

As part of the Voluntary Joint Committee for the Peak National Park, CPRE Peak District and South Yorkshire commissioned an engineering geologist to report on quarrying in the Peak District. The 1950 report included examples and diagrams of good quarries, which did not impact the landscape, and bad quarries, which did. The report recommended that existing quarries should continue to develop, however, these and new proposals should be controlled by the planning system.

More recently, the branch has lobbied the Peak District National Park Authority and the Campaign for National Parks (CNP) to amend and strengthen planning regulations around old quarry permissions. Around the turn of the century, the branch provided material for a national campaign coinciding with a government review of its policy on aggregates. Of particular concern was the continuing pressure on the Peak District to provide aggregates for road building.

The Minerals Campaign Group was created in 2000 to focus on quarrying. It worked to influence Derbyshire County Council's minerals strategy and campaigned to change planning guidance and against specific quarry proposals. The Old Minerals Permissions Project undertook research, which was shared nationally. As a result of joint campaigning with CNP, the government issued new laws in 2008 to bring all old mineral permissions under modern planning controls. This enabled the Branch to help stop limestone quarrying under the guise of fluorspar extraction at Longstone Edge. Further success in long-running cases was achieved on Stanton Moor. See Quarrying out the National Park – 2004 - 2013.

Eldon Hill

Eldon Hill Quarry. Copyright Peter Barr. Licensed for reuse under a Creative Commons Licence.

Eldon Hill is a limestone hill in the northern Peak District, between the villages of Castleton and Peak Forest. Permission to quarry was granted in 1950 after an unsuccessful CPRE Peak District and South Yorkshire campaign and a public inquiry. Much of the hill's northern and north-western slopes had been removed to provide a vast amount of limestone aggregate for road-building.

Over the next 40 years, there were three attempts to extend the quarry.

The first came in 1968 by Thomas W. Ward Roadstone of Sheffield, ironically a successor company to that founded by Ethel's father. They applied to the Peak Park Joint Planning Board, now the Peak District National Park Authority, to extend Eldon Hill Quarry and join it with Sparrowpit Quarry. CPRE Peak District and South Yorkshire leapt into action because the company wanted to completely remove the top of the hill and change the skyline forever. The Planning Board refused planning permission. The planners felt that the 'conspicuously sited quarry has already done serious damage... it would be wrong to allow any extension of working, however small, beyond the limits laid down in 1953.'

Ward's applied again to extend Eldon Hill Quarry in the 1980s. This time, they appealed on refusal and a public inquiry was held in Buxton. CPRE Peak District and South Yorkshire presented their case and the appeal was dismissed.

New owners, RMC Aggregates, applied once again to extend the quarry in 1995. The CPRE objected and the application was refused. In the same year, a member of the House of Lords called the quarry the best-known eyesore in the Peak District. This was during a debate on the need to restrict old mineral permissions granted between 1948 and 1981. As a result of CPRE Peak District and South Yorkshire and CNP campaigning, further planning restrictions were introduced in 2008.

The quarry closed in 1999 and now stands unused with vegetation starting to grow on the quarry faces.

Longstone Edge

RMC took over the 1950s mineral vein lease on Backdale Quarry, Longstone Edge, in 1996. This would be the start of a twenty-year campaign with the Save Longstone Edge Group (SLEG) and local communities that would finally come to a close in 2016.

CPRE Peak District and South Yorkshire worked closely with SLEG and the Campaign for National Parks, encouraging the Peak District National Park Authority to undertake enforcement action. Described as a 'test case for the Environment Act and for National Parks' the campaign fought hard and long, during which time vast quantities of limestone and minerals were removed. Stop notices, appeals and public inquiries raged during this period, involving a number of quarry companies.

Limestone quarrying ended in 2009 but the quarry operators kept up the pressure until 2016, when the final public inquiry relating to Longstone Edge cancelled the 1950s mineral planning permission.

Stanton Moor

One of the protestors, universally called 'eco warriors' at the time, who occupied Stanton Moor quarries.

A major quarry application to reopen the large dormant Endcliffe and Lees Cross Quarry on Stanton Moor was made in 1998, which led to a long-running planning controversy and campaign. CPRE Peak District and South Yorkshire worked with the Stanton Lees Action Group and Stanton in Peak Parish Council, while the site was notably occupied by protesters. In October 2001, the branch held a much-visited photographic exhibition in Bakewell, staged jointly with the Stanton Lees Action Group. In 2003 it published an expert planning consultants' report on the non-viability of the site.

Two separate planning applications were finally refused in 2008 and 2010.

You can read about the campaigns at Longstone Edge and Stanton Moor in Chapter 15 Quarrying out the National Park - 2004-2013.

Today

Old mineral permissions are no longer a threat to unrestricted quarrying in the Peak District thanks to CPRE Peak District and South Yorkshire lobbying that has resulted in the National Park Authority serving prohibition orders and national legislation bringing such permissions into modern planning controls. CPRE Peak District and South Yorkshire oppose fossil fuels, whether traditional fuels like coal or novel fuels such as fracked gas, because of the impact they have on climate change and the landscape.

15 | Quarrying out the National Park - 2004-2013

Backdale Quarry, Longstone Edge, June 2008.

The Situation

The continual scanning of planning applications, along with the ever-present threats of quarries, green belt development and major road building in the Longdendale Valley were the major ever-present issues that defined this decade. There was also a refresh of the campaign to underground electricity pylons and cables, and new campaigns to promote renewable energy and take motorised vehicles off green lanes.

Vast quantities of planning applications were scanned by the branch during this decade. In any one year, the branch could look at 18,000 applications, investigate between 300 and 900, and make submissions to the appropriate planning authority on anywhere from 30 to 100 cases. Some form of success was achieved with approximately 75% of submissions having positive impacts.

The ongoing large quarry planning applications on Longstone Edge and Stanton Moor were finally and successfully resolved.

Plans for the A628 Mottram-Tintwistle Bypass continued during this period and the branch worked hard to comment on numerous proposals. In 2013, the branch was concerned by new political pressure to promote the bypass.

'Keeping sites from harm' was a key phrase used by the branch as it opposed planning applications in green belts across the region. There were major proposals submitted in such places as the Hepworth's factory site and Loxley College – both in the Loxley Valley; Tween Bridge, Doncaster and Thorpe Hesley, Rotherham. The branch continued, unsuccessfully, to push Doncaster Council to extend the green belt to the east of the city by trying to get this as a local plan policy. This was one part of the work to protect green belts from adverse planning outcomes across South Yorkshire.

The branch brought small-scale renewable energy to the front of its agenda. It pushed the Peak District National Park Authority to relax its overly restrictive policy on renewable energy, arguing for more a proactive approach that would enable residents and businesses to install renewable energy schemes in keeping with requirements for landscape protection. As part of this, the branch launched a project to identify potential sites for micro-hydropower. By 2009, 150 possible sites had been identified and in-depth case studies prepared for 10. The branch ran community hydropower workshops and convened with the newly formed Peak Hydro Forum.

There was a renewed focus on the removal of pylons and overhead electricity cables by running them underground. National funding for transmission undergrounding was increased five-fold in 2012. The branch persuaded the local electricity companies to underground intrusive overhead lines across the region. Success was achieved at Blacka Moor, Hope, Sheldon and Wardlow among others. The branch also decided to pursue a campaign to remove pylons from Longdendale by underground cabling along the disused rail trackbed, overturning a long-standing branch policy of reopening the railway to reduce road traffic.

Part of the successful strategic work of the branch was to influence energy and minerals policies in Regional Spatial Strategy Panel Reports in Yorkshire and East Midlands.

The 'Take Back the Tracks' campaign against unsustainable and illegal off-roading was launched. Early successes for the campaign came when the PDNPA issued Traffic Regulation Orders to ban vehicles from green lanes such as Chapel Gate, Long Causeway and the Roych.

Source: *Based on Annual Reports.*

Some of our Achievements and Campaigns

Publications, Events and Local Plans

2010   Take Back the Tracks campaign launched to stop damaging and illegal off-roading.
2011   Barnsley, Doncaster, Peak District, Local Development Plans. The Branch submitted arguments at Examination in Public hearings to make the case for countryside protection and sustainable development.
2012   Buxton, Doncaster and Penistone, planning workshops for communities.
2012   Haythornthwaite Appeal launched.
2013   Peak District, Green Buildings Open Weekend, 20 sites showcased renewable energy and sustainable technology.

Green Belt Protection

2008   Woodhouse Junction, Network Rail maintenance facility refused.
2009   Thorne, after a strong campaign an outsized strategic warehouse was refused.
2009   Sheephouse Heights, Barnsley, five 125m wind turbines refused.
2009   Blackstone Edge, Barnsley, appropriately sited wind farm approved.
2013   High Speed 2 (HS2), began to review proposed route.

National Park Protection

2004   Eyam, 27 houses, coach park and sports centre refused.
2004   Foolow, Brosterfield Farm opencast fluorspar mine refused.
2006   Mottram-Tintwistle, persuaded Natural England, Peak District National Park Authority and 1,400 letter writers to oppose the bypass.
2006   Chinley Moor, building stone quarry approved to provide conservation grade stone.

2008   Stanton Moor, Endcliffe and Lees Cross large quarry extension refused.
2009   Longstone Edge, major limestone quarrying ends after a long campaign.
2010   Stanton Moor, New Pilhough large quarry extension refused.
2011   Chapel-en-le-Frith, 100 houses refused.
2011   Hartington, major development on site of cheese factory refused.
2011   Blacka Moor, electricity pylons moved underground.
2013   Chapel Gate, Long Causeway and the Roych, PDNPA ban motor vehicles with Traffic Regulation Orders.

How We Made a Difference
Longstone Edge

Backdale Quarry from Bank Wood, 2008.

CPRE Peak District and South Yorkshire had been involved with the campaign to save Longstone Edge since 1996 when quarry company RMC took over the lease on a 1950s planning permission to work the mineral veins. It then proceeded to remove huge amounts of limestone from the site by arguing this was necessary to get at the vein minerals. Unlawful limestone quarrying at Longstone Edge would become a major branch campaign, which increased in intensity in 2004.

This campaign began in 1996 when the branch attended public meetings and provided the Save Longstone Edge Group with extensive information and advice. As with other major campaigns, the branch worked on several fronts. It alerted the Council for National Parks, encouraged the Peak Park Authority to undertake enforcement action and lobbied Ministers. As a result, RMC ceased work.

However, the explosives, diggers and trucks returned in July 2003 when Merrimans took over quarrying the site, owned by Bleaklow Industries. The National Park Authority served an Enforcement Notice in December 2004, which was appealed and led to a public inquiry in September 2005. The branch, as the Friends of the Peak District, teamed with the Save Longstone Edge Group to make the case against quarrying at the inquiry.

The case took three years to resolve when, in 2007, the government Planning Inspector ruled that quarrying was unlawful and had to stop. He calculated that the ratio of limestone to fluorspar being extracted was 91:1. He ruled that far more limestone was being removed than was acceptable to gain access to the vein minerals. The ratio should be 2:1. He stated that mining permission at Backdale should focus on fluorspar and barytes rather than limestone. After a series of court appeals, quarrying eventually ended in 2009, though it took a public inquiry in 2016 to finally tear up the permission.

Source: *Based on Annual Reports.*

Stanton Moor

Major planning applications to extend or re-open dormant quarries exercised the branch throughout the decade. CPRE Peak District and South Yorkshire first worked with the Stanton Lees Action Group in 1998. The focus of the campaigns was on an extension at New Pilhough Quarry and the reopening of a quarry at Endcliffe and Lees Cross. Quarry companies submitted and resubmitted a series of planning applications over the years. These led to public protests, including protesters taking up residence on site, widespread media coverage, CPRE Peak District and South Yorkshire hosted public events and letter writing campaigns.

Left: Dale View and New Pilhough Quarries, copyright Stanton Lees Action Group.
Right: Lees Cross Quarry.

The branch strongly opposed the Peak District National Park Authority's use of 1990s legislation to remove old permissions by exchanging these for new ones where the Authority could create stronger restrictions. Though this seemed like a benefit to the national park, the branch opposed this strategy as being damaging to national park principles. Blockstone Ltd wanted to do this trade at New Pilhough where it had exhausted the area it was allowed to quarry. The company applied for new planning permission to quarry two fields and give up permission for nearby Dungeon Quarry, which it had bought to make the exchange. The branch opposed the application on the basis that new quarries should not be allowed in national parks. The Authority initially granted permission in 2001 but when the application had to be reviewed due to a technicality, the Authority refused it based on the arguments put forward by the branch. The company appealed and resubmitted, and the Authority once more granted permission in 2002. The same year, Stancliffe Stone applied to reopen Endcliffe and Lees Cross quarries near Nine Ladies Stone Circle, which had been dormant for over 40 years.

The campaign and joint work with the Stanton Lees Action Group and Stanton in Peak Parish Council culminated in major successes with the final resolution of the applications in 2008 and 2010, including an equitable swap for Endcliffe and Lees Cross.

Source: *Based on Annual Reports.*

16 | Energy – A Tale of Two Centuries
By Andy Tickle

Pylons at Dunford Bridge. Copyright Dave Bevis and licensed for reuse under a Creative Commons Licence.

Overhead Electricity

The need for energy and its impact on rural areas has been a longstanding theme for the branch. It reared its head with the passing of the 1926 Electricity (Supply) Act which recommended a 'national gridiron' system be created. As early as 1928, overhead electricity lines began to swarm up the Hope Valley and the branch lobbied hard to reduce impacts, getting lines placed underground near Grindleford (1929) and in Castleton, Bamford and Hope (1930).

Some major successes were scored: in 1949 forcing the re-routing of a pylon line to the east of Sheffield, instead of through the western green belt and Peak fringe. The climax of the 20th century successes came in the mid-60s when a pylon line between Yorkshire and Manchester was proposed, running through the national park between Dunford Bridge and Woodhead and thence down the magnificent Longdendale valley to Stalybridge. CPRE Peak District and South Yorkshire objected to pylons scarring the high moorland crossing between Dunford and Woodhead and, together with the Peak District National Park Authority, won the public inquiry; as a result, and at significant expense, the power cables were instead laid in the old Victorian railway tunnels on the Woodhead Line. This was a huge victory for amenity.

Campaigning against overhead wires revived in the early 2000s, initially prompted by Friends of the Lake District and Campaign for National Parks. The branch joined the national lobbying (by now of Ofgem, the government's electricity market regulator) and persistence won the day. From 2005 Ofgem createded an 'Undergrounding for Visual Amenity' (UVA) fund (applicable in national parks and AONBs) that electricity companies could voluntarily sign up for, with a five-yearly £70 million budget.

The branch, using specialist planning volunteers, partnered with the Peak District National Park Authority to survey areas of intrusive 'wirescapes' and nominate them for removal. Each year since then, many kilometres of poles and wires have been removed at iconic locations such as Blacka Moor (2011), Edensor (2013), the High Peak Trail (2014) and Magpie Mine (2022), benefiting amenity, biodiversity and the setting of major heritage assets. The success of the UVA project (still ongoing) has been a testament to persuasive local and national advocacy, public support and partnership working with the Peak District National Park Authority, Northern Powergrid, Electricity Northwest and National Grid Electricity Distribution.

Success also engendered success: emboldened by the early Ofgem campaign, the branch this time led national advocacy for a further fund for removing grid pylon lines in designated landscapes. As part of this campaign, in 2013 the branch - on behalf of CNP, Friends of the Lakes and the John Muir Trust - commissioned a specialist environmental economics assessment from Professor Richard Cowell (of Cardiff University), arguing that the proposed £100 million transmission undergrounding fund was insufficient. Ofgem caved in and announced £500 million would be available from 2015. The Peak benefitted directly with the removal (in 2022) of several kilometres of pylons that dominated Dunford Bridge (a key gateway to the Peak District) and the beautiful Trans Pennine Trail eastwards towards Penistone. Never taking 'no' for an answer, we are now lobbying again for the whole of Longdendale to be undergrounded.

Wind Power

An artist's impression of a turbine above Ball Eye quarry, seen from Stepping Lane, Bonsall. Copyright Christine Gregory.

Whilst windmills have traditionally been viewed benignly as part of the rural scene, their modern counterparts – wind turbines – have been far more controversial. With the ongoing climate emergency, few now dispute their role in helping the country meet its net zero targets. The question, as ever, is about appropriate scale and siting.

Turbines first raised their head locally in the early 1990s with proposals to build a wind farm at Royd Moor just outside Penistone. The branch objected (Gerald Haythornthwaite, not unsurprisingly, felt the structures to be deeply alien to the countryside). However, in hindsight, the turbines can be seen to be in relative harmony with the scale and openness of the enclosed pastoral Pennine landscape.

But as turbine size began to increase in the 2000s, some proposals had to be challenged. In part, and in the face of the need to meet national climate change targets, this required the branch to re-think its policy approach. The key lay in taking a strategic, regional approach to landscape capacity and being able to judge applications both in relation to how much renewable energy capacity was needed (and by when) in each local authority area and steering development (via the government's Regional Spatial Strategies) to the least vulnerable landscapes.

This gave a clear framework for the branch's approach – leading to support for windfarms that met the branch's criteria (e.g. Crow Edge in 2007, Spicer Hill, Hampole and Marr in 2008/9, Ulley near the M1 in 2013) although objecting where we believed major landscape damage was likely (Thorne Moors, lost at a major public inquiry in 2007). Whilst we supported small (Tideswell Moor) and even medium turbines in the national park (campaigning successfully in 2014 for two turbines near Parwich to support a family dairy farm), the branch continued to be vigilant opposing turbines that would dominate the edges and setting of the national park (applications refused at High Edge, Buxton in 2003; Sheephouse Heights above Midhopestones in 2009, Matlock Moor in 2010, and Griffe Grange near Longcliffe, the latter refused on appeal in 2016).

Positive Energy

As part of a more enlightened approach to rural renewables, the branch strove to promote – across the board – the most appropriate low carbon solutions, whether in the national park or elsewhere. It also showed the branch to be proactive in its campaigning, recognising that climate change is the biggest threat to the English countryside. In the 2000s this climaxed with a major project (funded by the Peak District National Park Authority's Sustainable Development Fund, SDF) on the potential of re-using old mills in the Peak for micro-hydropower. The five-year, volunteer-led survey identified some 150 new sites with development potential and produced outline feasibility studies for 10 of the most promising sites. The final report was launched in late 2010 at Cromford Mill by the leader of Derbyshire County Council with a glowing foreword contributed by the then Secretary of State for the Environment, Hilary Benn.

As a follow-up, the Peak Hydro Forum was formed to take forward community-led schemes; sadly, it folded after a number of years, mainly due to a hostile policy environment nationally where grant funding and subsidies (such as feed-in tariffs) were being repeatedly cut. Undaunted, the branch looked to other ways to promote green energy in the Peak and beyond and in 2013 – again with the help of the SDF – launched a 'Green Buildings Open Up' weekend and website, where the public could visit exemplar energy generation schemes and retrofitted buildings (either in person or via detailed case studies on the website).

Community energy visioning with Bonsall residents.

Following on from much work by the branch in the 2000s on promoting neighbourhood planning, we helped pioneer a new community-centred approach to rural renewables called 'community energy visioning' (CEV). First piloted by CPRE in North Yorkshire, the branch then rolled out the CEV project in Bonsall (working with CPRE Derbyshire) and Woodsetts in Rotherham. This was a 'bottom-up' approach to planning (rather than the usual developer-led imposition of energy schemes) where communities assessed their need for low carbon energy against local landscape capacity and their tolerance of change. The results were then turned into visualisations by talented local artists, Christine Gregory and Richard Johnson. The vision documents (published for Bonsall in 2022; Woodsetts in 2023) were then a template for each community to take forward detailed proposals. As a result, the newly-formed Bonsall Energy Group has now attracted a major government grant to scope a solar array in a local disused quarry.

Fittingly, in late 2023 the Bonsall and Woodsetts projects received a 'highly commended' award for community engagement and inclusion at the national Community Energy England awards. The branch is now working with National CPRE on a major UK Lottery application for further community energy vision rollout in 2025-26.

Today

The branch recognises the urgent need to address climate change and that, increasingly, this places our countryside under pressure to absorb new forms of sustainable energy, including wind turbines.

We remain very supportive of renewable energy, especially where it delivers benefits to local communities and the rural economy. We encourage local communities to come forward with their own plans for generating green energy. However, we are concerned that there's no strategic approach to planning the best places for windfarms and other forms of green power, so we lobby local authorities to be more proactive in mapping the countryside's capacity for change.

17 | Hard Campaigns and Happy Celebrations - 2014-2024

Removing vehicles from green lanes and promoting the Peak District National Park boundary were two major campaigns.

The Situation

Monitoring planning applications continued to be a major part of branch work. There was a similar success rate as the previous ten years, with the positive influence on applications even rising to 90% in 2017. As part of this work, the branch opposed several large housing developments across the region, sadly not always with success. Campaign work included setting out the case against approval, working closely with local communities and submitting evidence at public inquiries.

Fracking became a major issue in 2014, despite the government quickly clarifying that there would be no drilling in national parks. In 2016 the branch began a major campaign with a new policy against gas extraction in the local countryside. A national moratorium was announced in 2019 due to concerns about earthquakes, though this did not rescind the local trial drilling permissions. The government has now dropped its support for fracking altogether.

The Take Back the Tracks campaign to end off-roading by motorised vehicles on green lanes continued with a series of Traffic Regulation Orders. These banned motor vehicles on several lanes across the region, from Washgates in Staffordshire to Derby Lane near Monyash.

The work to underground electricity pylons and cables continued with many successes. The National Grid agreed to remove pylons east of Dunford Bridge near Woodhead Tunnel. The last pylon was taken down in 2022. Miles of unsightly overhead lines were removed across the region including at Chapel-en-le-Frith, Butterton, Glossop, Hope, Midhopestone, Moscar, Pobgreen and Redmires, among other locations.

The Northern Powerhouse became a new government strategy and the branch engaged with it to put the countryside at the heart of the North's economic future. The branch held high level meetings with MPs, including Patrick McLoughlin, then Secretary of State for Transport. Transport for the North was an important Powerhouse body, as it gained statutory powers as a transport body in 2018, and hence also a target for lobbying.

Transport remains an ever-constant issue. The branch took up a position to decarbonise transport and joined the Derbyshire Climate Coalition. It commented on the Northern Powerhouse proposal for a cross Peak District road tunnel and was disappointed that this was not to be a road and rail tunnel. In 2017, a short tunnel was chosen to be pursued with major upgrades to a dual carriageway for the A628 between the M67 and M1 with a new M1-M18 dual carriageway link. The branch objected to fresh Department of Transport plans for the A57 bypass of Mottram and extending it to Tintwistle, the first part of creating the longer M67 to M1 dual carriageway. It attended public inquiries in 2017 and 2021 to reinforce its views and took the government to judicial review at the High Court in 2023. The branch continued to press for a new rail link across the Pennines to reduce the need for upgrading the A628 to a dual carriageway. The proposed route of High Speed 2 was originally published in 2013. While the branch welcomed revised plans to direct the route along the M18 corridor, it lodged objections to the major impacts on landscape, tranquillity and wildlife along much of the route. This eastern leg was removed in 2021.

Commenting on local plans was a major part of core work from 2014 to 2018. The creation of local plans is a lengthy process and the branch engaged with the local authorities throughout. Representations were made on plans in Barnsley, Doncaster, High Peak, North East Derbyshire, Rotherham and Sheffield over several years. Within these, large-scale housing plans were fought and formal losses to the green belt in Barnsley and Rotherham were opposed. While not successful in some cases, the Sheffield Local Plan endorsed the option to confine development to the city area with minimal building in the green belt on brownfield sites.

Some of our Achievements and Campaigns

Publications, Events and Local Plans

2016 Peak District, community neighbourhood planning workshops.
2016 South Yorkshire, participation and advocacy in local plan making workshops.
2017 *Green Belt Blueprint* published. This was an advocacy document setting out the branch agenda for Sheffield's green belt.
2017 Peak District National Park Boundary Walk officially opened and the guidebook published.
2020 Sheffield, new green belt campaign launched against inappropriate housing.
2021 Longdendale, Car Free Low Carbon Travel for Longdendale public event.
2021 Peak District, 'Ethels' launched as the new collective name for the highest summits in the Peak District.
2024 Centenary celebrations.

Green Belt Protection

2017 Oughtibridge, successfully stopped the paper mill developer from removing affordable housing, which would have set a precedent for brownfield sites.
2018 Whaley Bridge, a large housing development refused.
2019 Buxton, 120 houses refused on Leek Road.
2019 Eckington, Harthill and Woodsetts, fracking proposals opposed at three public inquiries.
2021 Loxley, 300 houses on Hepworth's site were refused after a public inquiry following an appeal by the developer.

National Park Protection

2014	Great Hucklow, supported underground fluorspar mining to reduce pressure for opencast mining.
2014	Hurdlow to Parsley Hay, overhead electricity cables buried underground.
2015	Stanton Moor, noisy wire saws at Dale View Quarry refused.
2015	Chatsworth Park, two hydroelectric power schemes approved.
2016	Longstone Edge, the final public inquiry about Backdale Quarry resulted in the government cancelling the 1950s planning permission that had caused problems for 20 years. CPRE Peak District and South Yorkshire, PDNPA and Save Longstone Edge Group celebrated with a walk and picnic on the Edge.
2017	Washgates in Staffordshire, motorised vehicles banned except for historic motorcycle trials, which we supported.
2017	Derby Lane near Monyash, motorised vehicles banned with Traffic Regulation Order.
2019	Grindleford, Stoke Hall Quarry application withdrawn.
2019	Sterndale Moor, Buxton, Breedon quarry plans were significantly revised.
2019	Wetton, motorised vehicles banned with Traffic Regulation Order.
2019	Stoney Middleton, motorised vehicles banned on Jacob's Ladder with Traffic Regulation Order.
2022	Dunford Bridge, electricity pylons removed and cables put underground.
2023	Upper Derwent Valley, Severn Trent Water drop reservoir extension plans.

How We Made a Difference
Fracking

We campaigned to stop the government from fast-tracking fracking – and we won! Locally, and nationally, we ran a hard-hitting campaign opposing the government's plans to fast-track fracking through the planning system, over the heads of local people.

In 2017, we worked with communities and Friends of the Earth to oppose three applications for drilling at Eckington in North East Derbyshire, and Harthill and Woodsetts in Rotherham. Eckington and Harthill were refused

Community protestors outside Rotherham Town Hall after Rotherham Metropolitan Borough Council refused permission for fracking at Harthill.

in 2018, with INEOS lodging appeals. We helped communities prepare for public inquiries with training and support, which Eckington and Harthill sadly lost in 2018. Woodsetts was finally won in 2022. We worked with National CPRE to lobby against government plans to water down the planning system to make it easier to bypass local democracy. A moratorium was announced in 2019 due to concerns about earthquakes, though at the time this did not halt the three local applications. The government soon halted fracking altogether.

We argued that fracking was bad for the countryside, local communities and the environment – and in the end, common sense prevailed. The government has now dropped its support for fracking altogether: great news for communities and the countryside.

At a time when we need to cut down carbon emissions and reduce our reliance on fossil fuels, we remained vigilant to ensure that together with local people, we kept fighting against this unnecessary industrialisation of our countryside.

Hepworth's Site, Loxley Valley

The branch campaigned for three years with Friends of the Loxley Valley against the creation of a new suburb of 300 homes on the former site of Hepworth's factory.

We started with a public workshop in 2018 and tried to engage the developer as well as Sheffield City Council in finding a sustainable solution for the site. Sadly the developer did not listen and their damaging proposal galvanised almost a thousand people to object to the planning application. We worked with numerous local groups and spoke to the Sheffield Hallam and Hillsborough MPs, and local councillors, who also all objected.

The City Council unanimously rejected the planning application, because the development would damage green belt, landscape and ecology, including substantial tree loss: the site was clearly an unsustainable location for large-scale housing. The site owners, Patrick Properties, appealed against the decision, and a three-week-long planning inquiry followed.

The branch and Friends of the Loxley Valley played a major role in the inquiry, employing a barrister and expert witnesses. We told the Planning Inspector that the old factories do need cleaning up and restoration, but not in a way that causes more problems than it solves. The new suburb would dominate the beautiful

green belt valley bottom on the edge of the Peak District National Park and create an unsustainable isolated enclave, leaving hundreds of residents dependent on their cars for most of their everyday needs.

Planning Inspector Martin Whitehead agreed, ruling that the proposed development of 300 homes would substantially harm green belt countryside. He said it was in breach of national planning policy and would damage the special character of the Loxley Valley. He highlighted the Loxley River as an important 'Green Corridor' that required safeguarding.

He said the development would lead to an unacceptable loss of mature trees, and he was unconvinced that it would not damage ecology and biodiversity. These trees screen the old factory buildings but the development would urbanise and intensify activity on the site, altering its character by creating *"a suburban domestic setting that would visibly increase activity and* lighting and result in greater noise in the area both during the night and day. The proposal would be harmful to the special character of the Loxley Valley."

In 2024, Sheffield-based housing company Sky-House has announced plans to build around 60 single-storey houses on the site.

Peak District Boundary Walk

The Peak District Boundary Walk stage 4, Old Glossop to Greenfield. Copyright Mark Chadwick.

CPRE Peak District and South Yorkshire created the waymarked 190 mile circular Peak District Boundary Walk in 2017 to celebrate Britain's first national park.

Stretching from the moorland tops of the South Pennines to the gentle limestone scenery of the Derbyshire Dales, the route embraces the urban edges of Sheffield and Oldham, as well as Staffordshire's rugged moorland and the undulating slopes of Cheshire.

The route is almost identical to the national park boundary drawn up and proposed by our founders – Ethel and Gerald Haythornthwaite in the 1930s. A key ambition of the project was to take people to unsung, but equally beautiful, parts of the Peak, spreading visitor income more widely.

The *Peak District Boundary Walk* book is a guide to the route. It includes a detailed route description, Ordnance Survey 1:25,000-scale maps and information about places of interest and local facilities. The book also examines some of the key issues facing the national park and how the branch has campaigned to safeguard our most precious landscapes.

Ethels

Hen Cloud, Staffordshire. It is one of the 95 Ethels. Ethel Data. Height 410 metres. Prominence 60 metres. Map Data. Grid Ref SK008615. Copyright Steve Wood.

CPRE Peak District and South Yorkshire supporter Doug Colton came up with the idea for the 'Ethels' in 2021 as a tribute to Ethel Haythornthwaite.

The Ethels are all Peak District hilltops over 400 metres above sea level and some significant lower prominent hills that stand out in their own right. There are 95 in total.

They range from the 287 metre summit of Thorpe Cloud at the gateway to Dovedale in the limestone 'White Peak' to the remote moorland summits of Kinder Scout, Bleaklow and Black Hill in the northern gritstone 'Dark Peak' area. The highest is the top of Kinder Scout, at 636 metres above sea level.

Doug worked with us to create the app named 'Ethel Ready'. It can be downloaded for both Apple and Android phones.

Ethel Haythornthwaite is also celebrated in a major new biography by Helen Mort, published in 2024 as part of our centenary celebrations.

18 The Future

Although there are common threads running through much of the work of the charity over the last one hundred years (access, transport, planning, sustainable development, national parks, energy etc.) the social, economic and political environments in which we have striven to promote, enhance and protect the landscapes and green spaces of the Peak District and South Yorkshire have changed beyond all recognition.

The pressures on the countryside have never been greater nor has the urgency and importance of campaigning to protect it ever been more critical.

We have campaigned ceaselessly for a century as detailed in part in this account of our work. We shall continue to do so, but only if we can secure generous public support.

CPRE Peak District and South Yorkshire
Sheffield
May 2024

www.cprepdsy.org.uk

Presidents, Chairs, Honorary Secretaries & Honorary Treasurers

PRESIDENTS		CHAIRS	
Sir Henry Hadow, CBE	1924-37	Dr. William S. Porter	1924-25
Sir William Rothenstein, DLitt, MA, ARCA	1938-45	Dr. R. G. Abercrombie	1925-33
The Rt. Hon. Lord Chorley, QC	1946-74	Professor E. S. Forster, MBE, MA	1933-48
Sir Eric Mensforth, CBE, DL, FEng	1975-86	J. Mansell Jenkinson, FRIBA	1948-66
General Sir Hugh Beach, KCB, OBE, MC, MA, BSc	1987-98	S. E. Furey, LLB	1966-77
Lord Hardy of Wath	1998-03	C. A. Humphrey, MA	1977-80
Lord Hattersley of Sparkbrook	2003-08	G. D. C. Shaw, LLB	1980-92
Julia Bradbury	2008-15	A. D. W. Shepherd, Dip Arch	1992-99
Dame Fiona Reynolds	2015-24	Jack Burling	1999-02
		Anne Robinson	2002-07
		George Wolfe	2007-11
		Isabella Stone	2011-14
		John Lambert	2014-17
		Chris Heard	2017-20
		Julie Parry	2020-23
HONORARY SECRETARIES*		HONORARY TREASURERS	
Mrs. E. M. B. Haythornthwaite, MBE, MA (formerly Mrs. H. B. Gallimore)	1924-80	A. B. Ward, MA	1932-40
Lt. Col. G. G. Haythornthwaite, CBE, TD, MA, FRIBA, FRTPI	1980-95	Edward Bromley, LLD, MA, JP	1940-47
Jean Hodgkinson	1995-03	A. E. Irons	1947-81
		J. Derek Grayson, MA, LLB	1981-99
* SECRETARY TO THE TRUSTEES from 2000		Tom Dakin	1999-00
		Tony Willey	2000-04
		Chris Howard	2004-07
		Chris Sparshatt	2007-11
		John Layton	2011-12
		Isabel Hartland	2012-15
		Andy Brightmore	2016-18
		Paul Cooper	2019-20
		Eugene Walker	2021-24